# IN A
# LONELY
# PLACE

# THE BEST
# MYSTERIES
## OF ALL TIME

Dorothy B. Hughes's unforgettable 1947 novel *In a Lonely Place* is a crime fiction standout for several reasons. Most noteworthy was that the book was one of the first mysteries ever written from the criminal's point of view. Hughes chose to portray the inner thoughts of Dix Steele, her antihero, rather than focus on the innocent victims. The result was groundbreaking psychological suspense that gripped readers from page one. In addition, Hughes's spare, no-nonsense hard-boiled writing style echoes the male masters of noir such as Raymond Chandler and Dashiell Hammett rather than the cozy, gentler style of women crime writers of the era. Hughes, the 1978 Grand Master of the Mystery Writers of America, remains a truly outstanding contributor to America's all-time best mystery fiction.

# Other Crime Novels by
# Dorothy B. Hughes

# In A Lonely Place

## Dorothy B. Hughes

THE BEST
MYSTERIES
OF ALL TIME

ImPress • Pleasantville, New York

## THE BEST MYSTERIES OF ALL TIME

In a Lonely Place

ImPress is an imprint of The Reader's Digest Association, Inc., Bedford Road, Pleasantville, New York 10570.

ISSN 1544-4007

PRINTED IN THE UNITED STATES OF AMERICA

*For Charlotte*

*It's in a lonesome place you do have to be talking with someone,*
*and looking for someone, in the evening of the day.*

—J. M. Synge

# Chapter One

1

IT WAS good standing there on the promontory overlooking the evening sea, the fog lifting itself like gauzy veils to touch his face. There was something in it akin to flying; the sense of being lifted high above crawling earth, of being a part of the wildness of air. Something too of being closed within an unknown and strange world of mist and cloud and wind. He'd liked flying at night; he'd missed it after the war had crashed to a finish and dribbled to an end. It wasn't the same flying a little private crate. He'd tried it; it was like returning to the stone ax after precision tools. He had found nothing yet to take the place of flying wild.

It wasn't often he could capture any part of that feeling of power and exhilaration and freedom that came with loneness in the sky. There was a touch of it here, looking down at the ocean rolling endlessly in from the horizon; here high above the beach road with its crawling traffic, its dotting of lights. The outline of beach houses zigzagged against the sky but did not obscure the pale waste of sand, the dark restless waters beyond.

He didn't know why he hadn't come out here before. It wasn't far. He didn't even know why he'd come tonight. When he got on the bus, he had no destination. Just the restlessness. And the bus brought him here.

He put out his hand to the mossy fog as if he would capture it, but his hand went through the gauze and he smiled. That too was good; his hand was a plane passing through a cloud. The sea air was good to smell; the darkness was soft closed around him. He swooped his hand again through the restless fog.

He did not like it when on the street behind him a sudden bus spattered his peace with its ugly sound and smell and light. He was sharply angry at the intrusion. His head darted around to vent his scowl. As if the lumbering box had life as well as motion and would shrink from his displeasure. But as his head turned, he saw the girl. She was just stepping off the bus. She couldn't see him because he was no more than a figure in the fog and dark; she couldn't know he was drawing her on his mind as on a piece of paper.

She was small, dark-haired, with a rounded face. She was more than pretty; she was nice looking, a nice girl. Sketched in browns—the brown hair, brown suit, brown pumps and bag, even a small brown felt hat. He started thinking about her as she was stepping off the bus; she wasn't coming home from shopping, no parcels; she wasn't going to a party, the tailored suit, sensible shoes. She must be coming from work; that meant she descended from the Brentwood bus at this lonely corner every night at—he glanced to the luminous dial of his watch—seven-twenty. Possibly she had worked late tonight, but that could be checked easily. More probably she was employed at a studio, close at six, an hour to get home.

While he was thinking of her, the bus had bumbled away and she was crossing the slant intersection, coming directly towards him. Not to him; she didn't know he was there in the high foggy dark. He saw her face again as she passed under the yellow fog light, saw that she didn't like the darkness and fog and loneness. She started down the California Incline; he could hear her heels striking hard on the warped pavement as if the sound brought her some reassurance.

He didn't follow her at once. Actually he didn't intend to follow her. It was entirely without volition that he found himself moving down the slant, winding walk. He didn't walk hard, as she did, nor did he walk fast. Yet she heard him coming behind her. He knew she heard him for her heel struck an extra beat, as if she had half stumbled, and her steps went faster. He didn't walk faster; he continued to saunter, but he lengthened his stride, smiling slightly. She was afraid.

He could have caught up to her with ease, but he didn't. It was too soon. Better to hold back until he had passed the humped midsection of the walk, then to close in. She'd give a little scream, perhaps only a gasp, when he came up beside her. And he would say softly, "Hello." Only "Hello," but she would be more afraid.

She had just passed over the mid hump, she was on the final stretch of down grade. Walking fast. But as he reached that section, a car turned at the corner below, throwing its blatant light up on her, on him. Again anger plucked at his face; his steps slowed. The car speeded up the Incline, passed him, but the damage was done; the darkness had broken. As if it were a parade, the stream of cars followed the first car, scratching their light over the path and the road and the high earthen Palisades across. The girl was safe; he could feel the relaxation in her footsteps. Anger beat him like a drum.

When he reached the corner, she was already crossing the street, a brown figure under the yellow fog light marking the intersection. He watched her cross, reach the opposite pavement, and disappear behind the dark gate of one of the three houses huddled together there. He could have followed, but the houses were lighted; someone was waiting for her in the home light. He would have no excuse to follow to her door.

As he stood there, a pale blue bus slid up to the corner; a middle-aged woman got out. He boarded it. He didn't care where it was going; it would carry him away from the fog light. There were only a few passengers, all women, drab women. The driver was an angular, farm-looking man; he spun his change box with a ratcheting noise and looked into the night. The fare was a nickel.

Within the lighted box they slid past the dark cliffs. Across the width of the road were the massive beach houses and clubs, shutting away the sea. Fog stalked silently past the windows. The bus made no stops until it reached the end of that particular section of road, where it turned an abrupt corner. He got out when it stopped. Obviously it was leaving the sea now, turning up into the dark canyon. He stepped out, and he walked the short block to a little business section. He didn't know why until he reached that corner, looked up the street. There were several eating places, hamburger stands; there was a small drugstore, and there was a bar. He wanted a drink.

It was a nice bar, from the ship's prow that jutted upon the sidewalk to the dim ship's interior. It was a man's bar, although there was a dark-haired, squawk-voiced woman in it. She was with two men, and they were noisy. He didn't like them. But he liked the old man with the white chin whiskers behind the bar. The man had the quiet, competent air of a sea captain.

He ordered straight rye, but when the old man set it in front of him, he didn't want it. He drank it neat, but he didn't want it. He hadn't needed a drink; he'd relaxed on the bus. He wasn't angry with anyone anymore. Not even with the three noisy sons of bitches up front at the bar.

The ship's bells behind the bar rang out the hour, eight bells. Eight o'clock. There was no place he wanted to go, nothing he wanted to do. He didn't care about the little brown girl anymore.

4

He ordered another straight rye. He didn't drink it when it came; he left it there in front of him, not even wanting to drink it.

He could go across to the beach, sit in the sand, and smell the fog and sea. It would be quiet and dark there. The sea had appeared again just before the bus turned; there was open beach across. But he didn't move. He was comfortable where he was. He lit a cigarette and idly turned the jigger of rye upon the polished wood of the bar. Turned it without spilling a drop.

It was his ear caught the word spoken by the harsh-voiced woman. He wasn't listening to her, but the word spun, and he thought the word was "Brub." He remembered then that Brub lived out this way. He hadn't seen Brub for almost two years; he'd spoken to him only once, months ago when he arrived on the coast. He'd promised to let Brub know when he was settled, but he hadn't.

Brub lived in Santa Monica Canyon. He left his drink on the bar and went quickly to the phone booth in the corner. The book was tattered, but it was a Santa Monica book and there was the name, Brub Nicolai. He found a nickel and clanged it in the slot, asked the number.

A woman answered; he held on while she called Brub. Then Brub's voice, a little curious, "Hello."

He was excited just hearing the voice. There wasn't anyone like Brub, those years in England wouldn't have been real without Brub. He was gay as a boy, calling, "Hello there, Brub," wanting Brub to guess or to sense who it was. But Brub didn't know. He was puzzled; he asked, "Who's calling?"

Excitement titivated him. "Who do you think's calling?" he demanded. And he cried, "It's Dix. Dix Steele."

It was a good moment. It was the way he'd known it would be, Brub taking a gulp, then shouting, "Dix! Where you been hiding out? Thought you'd gone back East."

"No," he said. He was warm and comfortable in Brub's pleasure. "I've been sort of busy. You know how it is. Always something here. Something there."

"Yeah, I know." Brub asked, "Where are you now? What are you doing?"

"I'm sitting in a bar," he said, and heard Brub's answering crow. They'd spent most of their free time sitting in bars; they'd needed it in those days. Brub didn't know Dix no longer depended on liquor; he had a lot of things to tell Brub. Big brother Brub. "It's down by the ocean, has a ship's prow by the door—"

Brub had cut in. "You're practically here! We only live on Mesa Road, couple of blocks from there. Can you come up?"

"I'm practically there." He hung up, checked the street number in the phone book, returned to the bar, and swallowed the rye. This time it tasted good.

He was out on the street before he realized that he didn't have his car. He'd been walking up the street this afternoon, and he'd climbed on a Wilshire–Santa Monica bus, and he was in Santa Monica. He hadn't thought of Brub for months, and a scarecrow dame in a bar said what sounded like "Brub." She hadn't said it at all; she'd been calling the scarecrow guy with her "Bud," but he'd thought of Brub. Now he was going to see him.

Because it was meant to be, a taxi was held just then by the red light. At first he didn't recognize it as a cab; it was a dark, battered car with a young guy, hatless, driving it. It was empty. He read the lettering on it, "Santa Monica Cab Co.," even as the lights turned, and he ran out into the lonely street calling, "Hey, taxi."

Because it was meant to be, the driver stopped, waited for him. "Do you know where Mesa Road is?" His hand was on the door.

"You want to go there?"

"I sure do." He climbed in, still in his happiness. "Five-twenty."

The driver turned and drove back the way he'd come, a few blocks up the hill, a left turn and a steeper hill. The fog lay a deep and dirty white in the canyon; the windshield wiper pushed away the moisture. "This is Nicolai's," the driver said.

He was pleasantly surprised that the driver knew where he was going. It was a good omen; it meant Brub wouldn't have changed. Brub still knew everyone, everyone knew him. He watched the driver's fog lights circle, turn, and head down the hill. It was unconscious, the waiting and watching; in his thoughts was only the look of the amber swinging across the pillow of fog.

There was a gate to open; and the mailbox was white beside it. Lettered in black was B. Nicolai, 520 Mesa Road. He embraced the name. The house was high above the flowered terrace, but there was a light of welcome, amber as a fog light, in the front window. He climbed the winding flagstone steps to the door. He waited a second before he touched the brass knocker, again without consciousness, only a savoring of the moment before the event. He had no sooner touched it than the door was flung wide and Brub was there.

Brub hadn't changed. The same short-cut, dark, curly hair, the same square face with the grin on the mouth and in the shining black eyes. The same square shoulders and the look of the sea on him; he rolled like a sailor when he walked. Or like a fighter. A good fighter. That was Brub.

He was looking up at Dix, and his hand was a warm grip on Dix's hand. "Hello, you old son of a sea cook," he said. "What do you mean by not calling us before now? Let me see you."

He knew exactly what Brub saw, as if Brub were a mirror he was standing before. A young fellow, just an average young fellow. Tanned, medium light hair with a little curl, medium tall, and enough weight for height. Eyes, hazel; nose and mouth right for the face; a good-looking face but nothing to remember, nothing to set it apart from the usual. Good gabardine suit—he'd paid plenty to have it made—open-necked tan sports shirt. Maybe the face was sharpened at the moment by excitement and happiness, the excitement and happiness of seeing an old and favored friend. Ordinarily it wasn't one to remember.

"Let me look at you," he echoed. Brub was half a head shorter, and he looked down at Brub as Brub looked up at him. They made the survey silently, both satisfied with what they saw, both breaking silence together. "You haven't changed a bit."

"Come on in." Brub took his arm and ushered him out of the dim, pleasant hallway into the lighted living room. He broke step as they crossed the comfortable lamplighted room. Things weren't the same. There was a girl there, a girl who had a right to be there.

He saw her as he would always see her, a slender girl in a simple beige dress, curled in a large wing chair by the white fireplace. The chair was a gaudy piece patterned in greens and purples, like tropical flowers, with a scrawl of cerise breaking the pattern. Her hair was the color of palest gold, a silvery gold, and she wore it pulled away from her face into a curl at the back of her neck. She had a fine face, nothing pretty-pretty about it, a strong face with high cheek bones and a straight nose. Her eyes were beautiful, sea blue, slanted like wings; and her mouth was a beautiful curve. Yet she wasn't beautiful; you wouldn't look at her in a room of pretty women, in a bar or night spot. You wouldn't notice her; she'd be too quiet; she was a lady and she wouldn't want to be noticed.

She was at home here; she was mistress of the house, and she was beautiful in her content. Before either spoke, he knew she was Brub's wife. The way she was smiling as the two of them entered, the way her smile strengthened as Brub spoke. "This is Dix, Sylvia. Dickson Steele."

She put out her hand and finished the sentence, "Of whom I've heard you speak constantly. Hello, Dix."

Dix stepped forward to match her smile, to take her hand. Except for that first moment, he hadn't shown anything. Even that wouldn't have been noticed. "Hello, Sylvia," he said. She was tall standing, as tall as Brub. He held her hand while he turned to Brub, a prideful, smiling Brub. "Why didn't you tell me you were married?" he demanded. "Why hide this beautiful creature under the blanket of your indifference?"

Sylvia withdrew her hand, and Brub laughed. "You sound just like the Dix I've heard about," she retorted. She had a nice voice, shining as her pale hair. "Beer with us or whiskey as a stubborn individualist?"

He said, "Much to Brub's surprise, I'll take beer."

It was so comfortable. The room was a good one, only the chair was gaudy; the couch was like green grass and another couch the yellow of sunlight. There was pale matting on the polished floor; there was a big green chair and heavy white drapes across the venetian blinds. Good prints, O'Keeffe and Rivera. The bar was of light wood—convenient and unobtrusive in the corner. There must have been an ice chest; the beer was damp with cold.

Sylvia uncapped his bottle, poured half into a tall frosted glass and put it on an end table beside him. She brought Brub a bottle, poured a glass for herself. Her hands were lovely, slim and quiet and accurate; she moved quietly and with the same accuracy. She was probably a wonderful woman to bed with; no wasted motion, quietness.

When he knew what he was thinking, he repeated, "Why didn't you tell me you were married?"

"Tell you!" Brub roared. "You called me up seven months ago, last February, the eighth to be exact, told me you'd just got in and would let me know soon as you were located. That's the last I've heard of you. You checked out of the Ambassador three days later, and you didn't leave a forwarding address. How could I tell you anything?"

He smiled, his eyes lowered to his beer. "Keeping tabs on me, Brub?"

"Trying to locate you, you crazy lug," Brub said happily.

"Like the old days," Dix said. "Brub took care of me like a big brother, Sylvia."

"You needed a caretaker."

He switched back. "How long have you been married?"

"Two years this spring," Sylvia told him.

"One week and three days after I got home," Brub said. "It took her that long to get a beauty-shop appointment."

"Which she didn't need," Dix smiled.

Sylvia smiled to him. "It took him that long to raise the money for a license. Talk of drunken sailors! He spent every cent on flowers and presents and forgot all about the price of wedding."

Comfortable room and talk and beer. Two men. And a lovely woman.

Brub said, "Why do you think I fought the war? To get back to Sylvia."

"And why did you fight the war, Mr. Steele?" Sylvia's smile wasn't demure; she made it that way.

"For weekend passes to London," Brub suggested.

He stepped on Brub's words, answering her thoughtfully. He wanted to make an impression on her. "I've wondered about it frequently, Sylvia. Why did I or anyone else fight the war? Because we had to isn't good enough. I didn't have to when I enlisted. I think it was because it was the thing to do. And the Air Corps was the thing to do. All of us in college were nuts about flying. I was a sophomore at Princeton when things were starting. I didn't want to be left out of any excitement."

"Brub was at Berkeley," she remembered. "You're right. It was the thing to do."

They were steered to safe channels, to serious discussion. Brub opened another beer for the men.

Brub said, "It was the thing to do, or that was the rationalization. We're a casual generation, Dix; we don't want anyone to know we bleed if we're pricked. But self defense is one of the few prime instincts left. Despite the cover-up, it was self defense. And we knew it."

Dix agreed, lazily. You could agree or disagree in this house. No one got his back up, whatever was said. There was no anger here, no cause for anger. Even with a woman. Perhaps because of the woman. She was gentle.

He heard Sylvia's amused voice as from afar, as through a film of gray mist. "Brub's always looking for the hidden motive power. That's because he's a policeman."

He came sharply into focus. The word had been a cold spear deliberately thrust into his brain. He heard his voice speak the cold, hard word. "Policeman?" But they didn't notice anything. They thought him surprised, as he was, more than surprised, startled and shocked. They were accustomed to that reaction. For they weren't jesting; they were speaking the truth. Brub with an apologetic grin; his wife with pride under her laughter.

"He really is," she was saying.

And Brub was saying, "Not a policeman now, darling, a detective."

They'd played the scene often; it was in their ease. He was the one who needed prompting, needed cue for the next speech. He repeated, "Policeman," with disbelief, but the first numbing shock had passed. He was prepared to be correctly amused.

Brub said, "Detective. I don't know why. Everyone wants to know why, and I don't know."

"He hasn't found the underlying motive yet," Sylvia said.

Brub shrugged. "I know that one well enough. Anything to keep from working. That's the motto of the Nicolais. Graven on their crest."

"A big healthy man reclining," Sylvia added.

They were like a radio team, exchanging patter with seemingly effortless ease.

"My old man was a land baron, never did a lick of work. But land baroneering is outmoded, so I couldn't do that. The girls all married money." He fixed Sylvia with his eye. "I don't know why I didn't think of that. Raoul, my oldest brother, is an investment broker. That's what it says on his gold-lettered office door. Investment broker."

"Brub," Sylvia warned, but she smiled.

"Up and to the office by ten," Brub proclaimed. "Maybe a bit after. Open the mail. To the club for two quick games of squash. Shower, shave, trim, and lunch. Leisurely, of course. A quiet nap after, a bit of bridge—and the day's over. Very wearing."

Brub took a swallow of beer. "Then there's Tom—he plays golf. A lawyer on the side. He only takes cases dealing with the ravages of pterodactyls to the tidelands. The pterodactyls having little time for ravaging the tidelands, he has plenty of time for golf." He drank again. "I'm a detective."

Dix had listened with his face, a half smile, but he kept his eyes on his beer glass. His mouth was sharp with questions; they were like tacks pricking his tongue. Brub had finished and was waiting for him to speak. He said easily, "So you took the easy job. No investments or law for you. Sherlock Nicolai. And were you right?"

"No, damn it," Brub wailed. "I work."

"You know Brub," Sylvia sighed. "Whatever he does, he does with both heads. He's full fathoms deep in detecting."

Dix laughed, setting down his beer glass. It was time to go. Time to put space between himself and the Nicolais. "Brub should have taken up my racket." To their questioning eyebrows, he elucidated, "Like ninety-three and one-half percent of the ex-armed forces, I'm writing a book."

"Another author," Sylvia mused.

"Unlike ninety-two and one-half percent, I'm not writing a book on the war. Or even my autobiography. Just trying to do a novel." A wonderful racket; neither of them knew what a smart choice he'd made. Not haphazardly, no. Coldly, with sane reasoning. He stretched like a dog, preliminary to rising. "That's why you haven't seen me before. When you're trying to write, there isn't time to run around. I stick pretty close to the old machine." He smiled frankly at Brub. "My uncle is giving me a year to see what I can do. So I work." He was on his feet. He had meant to ask the use of the phone, to call a cab. But Brub wouldn't allow it; he'd insist on taking him to the bus line; he'd want to know where Dix was living. Dix didn't mind a walk. He'd find his own way to town.

He said, "And I'd better be getting back on the job."

They demurred, but they didn't mind. They were young and they were one, and Brub had to get up in the morning. He slipped the question in sideways. "After all, Brub has to have his rest to detect for the glory of Santa Monica, doesn't he?"

"Santa Monica! I'm on the L.A. force," Brub boasted mildly.

He'd wanted to know; he knew. The L.A. force.

"Then you do need sleep. Plenty of work in L.A., no?"

Brub's face lost its humor, became a little tired. "Plenty," he agreed.

Dix smiled, a small smile. Brub wouldn't know why; Brub had been his big brother, but he hadn't known everything there was to know. Some things a man kept secret. It was amusing to keep some things secret.

"I'll be seeing you," he said easily. His hand opened the door. But he didn't get away.

"Wait," Brub said. "We don't have your number."

He had to give it. He did without seeming reluctance. Brub would have noticed reluctance. Brub or the clear-eyed woman behind him, watching him quietly. He gave his telephone number, and he repeated his good-night. Then he was alone, feeling his way off the porch and down the path into the darkness and the moist opaque fog.

## 2

HE WALKED into the night not knowing the way, not caring. He'd moved more than once during his seven months in California. He could move again. It wasn't easy to find quarters, the right ones for him. He liked the place he had now; he'd been lucky about it. A fellow he'd known years ago, in college. Years, aeons ago. He hadn't cared for Mel Terriss then; he'd cared even less for him on running into him that night last July. Terriss was going to pouches; under his chin and eyes, in his belly. He had alcoholic eyes, and they were smearing the blonde with Dix. He didn't get an introduction. But he blatted waiting for it, and Dix had found the flat he'd been waiting for. He was sick and tired of the second-rate hotel off Westlake Park. It smelled. Terriss was telling everyone about being off to Rio for a year, a fat job to go with his fat head.

He could move again, but he was damned if he would. He liked Beverly Hills; a pleasant neighborhood. A safe neighborhood. It was possible he could change his phone number, Terriss's number. Get an unlisted one. He'd considered that before now. But Terriss's number was as good as being unlisted. There was no Dix Steele in the book.

Automatically he walked out of the small canyon, down to the beach road. He crossed to the ocean side; he could hear the crash of waves beyond the dark sands. He considered walking back along the waterfront, but sand walking was difficult and he was all at once tired. He turned in the direction of the Incline. There was no bus, no taxi, and no car stopped for him. He walked on, in the street most of the way because there was no sidewalk, keeping close to the buildings because in the fog he was no more than a moving blur. He was damned if he'd move or even bother to change his number. He didn't have to see Brub and his woman again. He'd proffered his excuse before it was needed. He was writing a book; he had no time for evenings like this, gab and beer.

He walked on, quiet as the fog. It had been pleasant. It was the first pleasant evening he'd had in so long. So terribly long. He tried to remember how long. Those early days in England when he and Brub knew each other so well.

He hardened his jaw, and he trudged on towards the yellow ring of fog light on the pavement ahead. He watched the light, watched it come closer as he moved silently towards it. He shut out thought, clamping it between his set teeth. It wasn't until he reached the light that he saw the Incline looming slantly across. And realized that the house into which the brown girl had disappeared lay just beyond. He stopped there, in the shadow of the clubhouse. The club's parking lot, wire-fenced, empty of cars, lay between him and the huddle of houses. The pounding of the sea recurred in changeless rhythm, and he could smell the salt far beyond the wire fence.

He had to walk up to the three houses; that was where the white lanes of the crosswalk lay on the highway. He smiled a little as he started forward. He was halfway past the fenced lot when the hideous noise of an oil truck, ignoring the stop sign, thundered past. A second one speeded after the first, and a third, blasting the quietness with thumping wheels, clanging chains. Spewing greasy smoke into the fog. He stood there trembling in anger until they passed. He was still trembling when he reached the huddle of houses, and when he saw what he saw, his anger mounted. There was no way to know beyond which brown gate the brown girl had vanished. The gates of the first and second houses stood side by side. Abruptly he crossed the street and started up the Incline. He had been so certain she had entered the center house. And now he didn't know. He'd have to watch again.

He was to the midsection, to the hump of the walk, before he was calmed again. He stopped there and looked out over the stone railing. There was a small replica of the Palisades on this other side of the railing. And here, just over the rail, was a broken place in the wild shrubbery, even the pressure of a footpath down the cliff. A place where a man could wait at night. He smiled and was easy again.

He walked on up the Incline, undisturbed when a car heading downwards splashed light on him. He wouldn't move from Terriss's flat. He was satisfied there. There was something amusing about Brub Nicolai being able to lay hands on him whenever he wished. Amusing and more exciting than anything that had happened in a long time. The hunter and the hunted arm in arm. The hunt sweetened by danger. At the top of the Incline he looked back down at the houses and the sand and the sea. But they were all helpless now, lost in the fog.

He went on, not knowing how he would get back to Beverly, not caring. He was surprised crossing to Wilshire to see the lights of a bus approaching. He waited for it. It was the Wilshire–L.A. bus. After he boarded it, he saw by his watch that it was still early, a little past eleven o'clock. There were only two passengers, working men in working clothes. Dix sat in the front seat, his face turned to the window. Away from the dull lights of the interior. Others boarded the bus as it rumbled along Wilshire through Santa Monica, into Westwood. He didn't turn his head to look at the others, but he could see their reflections in the window pane. There was no one worth looking at.

The fog thinned as the bus left Westwood and hurried through the dark lane framed by the woodland golf course. At Beverly you could see street corners again, as through a gray mesh. You could see the shopwindows and the people on the streets. Only there were no people, the little city was as deserted as a small town. Dix kept his face pressed to the window.

At Camden Drive he saw her. A girl, an unknown girl, standing alone, waiting alone there, by the bench, which meant a crosstown bus would eventually come along. At night busses didn't run often. Dix pulled the buzzer cord, but he was too late for Camden. He got off at the next stop, two blocks away. He didn't mind much. He crossed the boulevard, and he was smiling with his lips as he started back. His stride was long; his steps were quiet.

# 3

THE phone was a jangle tearing sleep from a man's face. It was the scream of bus brakes, the clanging chain of an ugly oil truck on a beach road, the whine of a spiraling bomb. Dix opened his cramped eyes. He didn't know how long the phone had been ringing. It stopped when his eyes opened, but as soon as he'd closed them again, the fretful noise began anew. This time he didn't open his eyes. With his outstretched hand he knocked the phone from its cradle, ending the sound. He buried his head in the pillow, grasped at waning sleep. He didn't want to talk to anyone this early. He didn't care who was on the other end of the phone. No one important. No one important had his number.

His eyes reopened. He'd forgotten Brub Nicolai. He'd given Brub his phone number last night. For a solitary moment the coldness of fear gripped his entrails. As quickly, the moment passed. He was without fear. But sleep had gone. He turned his head to look at the bedside clock. It wasn't so early. Eleven thirty-five. He'd had almost eight hours' sleep.

He needed eight hours more. God knows he needed it. He'd fallen into bed in complete exhaustion. It took more than eight hours to refuel a body exhausted. But his curiosity could not let him return to sleep now. He shoved away the covers and pulled on his bathrobe. He didn't bother with his slippers. He walked barefoot through the living room to the front door, opened it, and brought in the morning *Times* from his doorstep. His hands were eager, but he closed the door before opening the paper.

There was nothing unusual on the front page. The ways of civilization, international and national strife, wars and strikes, political propagandizing. Nothing he was expecting on the second page. That meant there'd be nothing. He thrust the paper under his arm. There'd been no reason to leave his bed. But now that he was up, he wanted coffee. He padded to the kitchen. Terriss had good stuff; he plugged in the electric percolator and opened the kitchen door to bring in the cream. The apartment was a corner one, easy for a man to keep to himself and to hold his affairs his own. No snoopy neighbors here. Most of them were connected with the studios; Terriss had told him that, told him with Terriss's fathead pride. They kept themselves private too.

While he was waiting for the coffee, he began to read the paper. He drank three cups, finishing his reading. He left the spread paper and the coffee cup on the kitchen table. There was maid service; he made it a point to be out during that period. The maid was a shapeless sack with heavy feet. She came to this apartment between two and three in the afternoon. He didn't know the maid's name; he wouldn't have recognized her on the street.

He returned to the bedroom. There wouldn't be time for good sleep before she came plodding in. If he were asleep, she wouldn't do the bedroom, and he didn't like an unmade bed. He sat down on the edge of it, noticed the phone, and replaced it in the cradle. He just sat there for minutes, not thinking, not seeing. Then he got up and went into the bathroom. His face in the mirror was the usual face, drawn from sleep, his hair rumpled. He'd feel better after a shower and a shave. He was taking his razor from the case when the phone rang.

He wasn't going to answer it, and then the quickening of curiosity stirred him. He took his time returning to it. Again he sat down on the rumpled bed. His hesitation before lifting the phone was so minute his hand didn't realize it. He said, "Hello."

"Dix?"

It was a woman's voice, a woman querying, "Dix?"

He took a breath. Only one woman could be calling. Sylvia Nicolai. He forced life into his voice. "Speaking. Sylvia?" He'd surprised her.

"How did you know?"

"Recognized your voice," he said amusedly. She would believe him.

"Where have you been? I've been trying all morning to reach you."

He didn't like having to account. Nor did she care; it was conversational gambit. Because he didn't like it, he lied. "I've been right here. Working. Phone didn't ring."

She said, "Phones," then went on in her cool, lovely voice, "Brub and I wondered if you'd like to join us for dinner at the club tonight?"

He didn't know what to say. He didn't know whether he wanted to be with them or not tonight. He was tired, too tired for decision. It was always easy to lie, so easy. He asked, "Could I ring you back, Sylvia? I've a tiresome date tonight, business. If I can get free of it, I'd much rather join you." The charm was in his voice; he turned it on. But she didn't match it. She was businesslike, as if she were Brub's secretary, not his wife. As if she preferred his refusal. "Yes, do call back. If you can't make it, we'll try it another time."

He echoed her good-bye and set back the phone. She didn't want him along tonight. It was Brub's idea and she'd said, "If you want him, Brub," because she was in love with Brub; the new hadn't been rubbed off their marriage. He wouldn't go. He wouldn't intrude on their oneness. They had happiness, and happiness was so rare in this day of the present. More rare than precious things, jewels and myrrh. Once he'd had happiness, but for so brief a time; happiness was made of quicksilver. It ran out of your hand like quicksilver. There was the heat of tears suddenly in his eyes, and he shook his head angrily. He would not think about it, he would never think of that again. It was long ago, in an ancient past. To hell with happiness. More important was excitement and power and the hot stir of lust. Those made you forget. They made happiness a pink marshmallow.

He stood up again, rubbing his untidy hair. He wouldn't go out with the Nicolais to their lace-panty club. He'd go out alone. The lone wolf. There was a savage delight in being a lone wolf. It wasn't happiness. It was the reverse of the coin, as hate was the reverse of love. Only a thin press of metal between the sides of a coin. He was a lone wolf; he didn't have to account to anyone, nor did he intend to. Sylvia Nicolai wanting to know where he was this morning. It was none of her damn business. This morning she didn't care, but get mixed up with the Nicolais and she would care. Women were snoopy. He hated women. Brub would be snoopy too; he was a detective.

Yet the game would be heightened if he teamed up with a detective. Dix went into the bathroom, plugged in the razor, and began to shave. Hating the noise, the grinding buzz of noise. He could have used a safety razor, but there were mornings when his hands had the shakes. He didn't know when those mornings would occur. Better the buzz than to have people noticing the cuts on your cheeks and chin. His hands were steady as iron this morning.

He finished shaving as quickly as possible, scrubbed his teeth, and sloshed mouthwash. He was feeling better. Under the shower he felt considerably better. It might be definitely amusing to be with the Nicolais tonight. It might be that Sylvia was the one who wanted him along, that her play of indifference was a cover-up. He was clinically aware of his appeal to women. He'd seen their eyes sharpen as they looked at him. Sylvia's hadn't, true, but she was smart. She wouldn't let it happen with Brub there. He'd like to see Sylvia again.

He thought of her as he stood scrubbing himself with the towel. The long lines of her, the silvery look and sound of her. He'd like to know a woman of her caliber. Brub was lucky. He flung the towel on the floor. Brub was born lucky. For an instant he stiffened, as if a cold hand had touched his spine.

His laugh shot from his throat. He was lucky too; he was more than lucky—he was smart. He strode out of the bathroom. It was close to two; he'd have to hump it to get out before the ugly beldame of the brooms showed up.

He put on a blue sports shirt, blue slacks, comfortable loafers. No jacket. From the open windows he knew the day was a sultry one. September was summer in California. He transferred his wallet and keys and other stuff from the crumpled gabardines he'd worn last night. He rolled the gabardines, opened his closet, and gathered up the other suits and odd trousers needing a cleaner's attention. He'd beaten the maid; he was ready to leave. The phone started to ring as he reached the front door. He ignored it and left the apartment.

The garages were in back of the court. His was almost a half block away. Just another of the advantages of Terriss's quarters. No insomniacs sitting up in bed checking you in and out. The garages fronted on an alley; a vacant lot across. He unlocked the one housing Terriss's car. A nice car Terriss had left for his use. He'd have preferred something flashier, a convertible or open brougham, but there was advantage in a black coupe. All black coupes looked alike at night. He drove away.

He dropped the bundle of clothes at the cleaner's on Olympic, then drove leisurely up Beverly Drive, parking near the delicatessen. He was hungry. He bought an early edition of the *News* at the corner, and he read it while he ate two smoked turkey sandwiches and drank a bottle of beer. The delicatessen was fairly crowded even this late. It was a popular place and a pleasant one. Noise was a blur here, like in a club.

There was nothing in the paper. After checking the headlines, he read the comics, the café columnists, and Kirby, Weinstock, and Pearson, loitering with his beer. He looked over the movie ads. Sometimes he went to a movie in the afternoons. It was too late today. He had to phone Sylvia Nicolai.

He walked down to the Owl after eating and bought a carton of Philip Morris. It was after three then. The beldame would be out of his apartment; he could return, call Sylvia, and catch a nap before joining the Nicolais at their club. The afternoon heat and the beer had made him sleepy again. Or he could get the letter written to Uncle Fergus. Damned old fool expected a letter once a week. It had been two weeks since Dix had written him. He wouldn't put it past Uncle Fergus to stop sending checks if he didn't get his damn letter from Dix pretty soon. He'd say he'd been sick. Maybe he could jack up the income for medical expenses. Something needing treatment, something acquired overseas. A back or a kidney. Not anything that would jerk the strings, drag him back East.

He got in his car, backed out, and drove a little too fast around the block. Uncle Fergus didn't have to be so dirty cheap; he didn't have another living relative. Two hundred and fifty a month was pennies. Medical treatment was a good idea. He should have thought of it before. He could get three hundred for sure, maybe three fifty. He'd write a whale of a letter. He was the boy could do it. He knew Uncle Fergus like the palm of his hand. He felt all hopped up returning to the apartment.

He flung the Philip Morrises on the divan, got out the portable, and opened it on the desk. He rolled in the paper and started, "Dear Uncle Fergus," before he remembered the phone call to Sylvia. He left the desk and went to the bedroom. Before dialing—

Terriss had extended service of course, Terriss had everything easy—he lit a cigarette.

Sylvia answered the phone. Her hello was natural. When he said, "Sylvia? It's Dix," her voice became a bit more formal. She was conscious of him all right. She was fighting that consciousness. He'd played the game so often of breaking down that withdrawal but never with this variation, the wife of his best friend. It stimulated him.

He asked, "Do you still want me tonight?"

She was conscious of his phrasing because there was a minute hesitancy before she counter-asked, "You mean you can join us for dinner?"

"If I'm still invited."

"Yes, indeed." She acted pleased. "Can you make it about seven? That will give us time for a drink before we go to the club."

"I'll be there."

He was pleased that he had decided to go. He lay back on the bed to finish his cigarette. He was still leisurely there when the phone sounded. He was surprised, more so when it was Sylvia again. Her voice wasn't standoffish now. "Dix? I forgot to say, don't dress. We're informal at the beach."

"Thanks," he said. "You eased my mind. My dinner coat is out at the seams. It shrank while I was away flying."

"Brub's too. They fed you gentlemen altogether too well," she laughed.

They had some easy conversation before ringing off. He didn't want to return to the damn typewriter. He was comfortable here on his spine; he wasn't sleepy now, just restful. It was just such delaying tactics that had let two weeks go by without writing the old skinflint. He pushed himself up and returned to the machine. Today there was incentive. He needed money for medical treatments.

DOROTHY B. HUGHES

Inspiration returned to him at the typewriter. He wrote a peach of a letter; it was just right, not too much nor too little. He didn't ask for money. He was certain his back would be all right without the treatments the doctor ordered. Stuff like that. He reread the letter twice before putting it in the envelope. He decided to go and mail it now. It was a little after five. Before sealing the envelope, he drew the letter out and read it again. Yes, it was right. He sealed it quickly, put on an airmail stamp, and left the apartment.

He was walking fast. That was why he didn't see the girl until he almost collided with her at the arched street entrance of the patio. It shocked him that he hadn't noticed her, that he hadn't been aware. He stepped back quickly. "I beg your pardon," he said. It wasn't a formality as he said it; shock made each word apology for a grave error.

The girl didn't move for a moment. She stood in his way and looked him over slowly, from crown to toe. The way a man looked over a woman, not the reverse. Her eyes were slant, her lashes curved long and golden dark. She had red-gold hair, flaming hair, flung back from her amber face, falling to her shoulders. Her mouth was too heavy with lipstick, a copper-red mouth, a sultry mouth painted to call attention to its premise. She was dressed severely, a rigid, tailored suit, but it accentuated the lift of her breasts, the curl of her hips. She wasn't beautiful—her face was too narrow for beauty—but she was dynamite. He stood like a dolt, gawking at her.

After she'd finished looking him over, she gave him a small insolent smile. As if he were a dolt, not Dix Steele. "Granted," she said, and she walked past him into the patio.

He didn't move. He stood and watched her, his mouth still open. She walked like a model, swaying her small buttocks. She had exquisite legs. She knew he was watching her and she didn't care. She expected it. She took her time, skirting the small sky-blue oblong

24

of the pool which lay in the center of the patio. She started up the stairway to the balcony of the second-floor apartments.

He swung out the archway fast. He wouldn't let her reach the balcony, look over the balustrade, and see him standing there. He'd find out about her some other way, if she lived here or whom she visited. He'd left his car down the block a bit, by the curb. Although he'd intended driving to the Beverly post office to mail the letter, he didn't. He half ran across the street to the corner mailbox, clanged in the letter, and ran back to the court. He was too late. She was already out of sight.

He went back into his own apartment, sauntered in as if he weren't damning luck. If he'd bumped into her on his return from the box, he could have bungled at his doorway for the key, discovered which apartment she entered. He walked inside, slamming the door after him. It had been years since he'd seen a girl who could set him jumping. The redhead was it. He went out to the kitchen, and although he didn't want a drink, he poured a double jigger of rye and drank it neat. The slug calmed him, but he wandered back into the front room, wanting an excuse to slip out into the patio, to look up at the second-floor balcony.

The excuse came as he wished for it. He heard, just short of the doorstep, the thud of the flung newspaper. He moved quick as a cat. But as soon as he picked up the paper, unfolding it, he forgot why he'd hurried outdoors. He saw only the headline: STRANGLER STRIKES AGAIN.

# Chapter Two

## 1

It was quarter past seven when Dix pulled up in front of Nicolai's gate. There was no woolly fog tonight; only a thin mistiness lay in the canyon. It was like gauze across the windshield. He could see the flagstoned steps clearly, even the geranium border framing them. The windows of the house were golden with light; the porch light was also on to welcome him.

He was again pleased that he had decided to come. He had dressed for deliberate effect, an Eastern friend of the Nicolais, well off, the right background, even to ex-Air Corps. Gray flannel suit; an expensive tie, patterned in navy, maroon, and white; a white shirt; well-polished brown shoes, English shoes. He settled his tie before climbing to the porch. He didn't hesitate before ringing the bell, and there was no hesitation in the opening door.

Sylvia was standing in the doorway. She had on her coat, a soft blue coat, and her bag, a white envelope, was under her arm. "Hello, Dix," she said. "I'll be right with you."

She didn't ask him in; the screen door was between them, and she didn't push it open. She left him standing there on the lighted porch while she turned back into the hall and switched off some overhead lights. There was dim light still glowing in the hall and living room when she came outside.

"We're meeting Brub at the club," she said in her high, clear voice as she started down the steps. "He called and asked me to bring you there for drinks. He couldn't make it home."

He followed her. He had to raise his voice to speak to her, she was that far ahead of him. She was accustomed to the steps; he must watch them. "Brub pretty busy?"

"Yes," she said, but she didn't continue on that. "Do you want to take your car or mine? It isn't far, only a few blocks."

She wasn't talking particularly fast, yet there was a breathlessness to it, as if she didn't want any silence between them, as if she were too conscious of him. She stood there by his car, tall and cool and lovely, but not quiet as she was last night.

He smiled at her; he put no intimacy into the smile. "We might as well take mine—it's here. You can direct me."

"All right," she agreed.

He helped her in and went around, took his place at the wheel. She'd rolled the window down on her side, and she rested her arm on the frame. She remained there in the far corner as she gave directions. "Just down to the beach road, turn left. The club's on the ocean side."

It didn't take five minutes to get there, no time for the furthering of acquaintance. She talked of club friends, names he didn't know. There was no silence on the short ride. On direction, he drove through the pillared gateway into the parking court. She let herself out of the car, not waiting for him to help her.

The clubhouse wasn't large. There was a young feel to it, like an officers' club. The couples in the entrance hall, in the lounge beyond, were the kind you'd expect the Nicolais to know. A pattern you found all over the country—decent, attractive young people. The norm. They didn't look dull to Dix tonight. He was warmed by their safeness.

Sylvia said, "I'll drop my coat." She smiled at him, an open, friendly smile. "Be right back, Dix."

She wasn't long. She looked lovely. Her dress was cream color, an expensively simple dress. He had pride entering the lounge with her.

"Brub doesn't seem to have shown up yet. Unless he's beaten us to the bar." She nodded to several couples as they crossed the room. There were more couples in the nautical bar, but Brub wasn't there. "I'll substitute for Brub and buy you a drink while we wait," she said.

"I approve the substitution. But I'll buy the drink," he told her.

She moved away from him to a table. "You can't. Not at the club. This is Brub's party."

She introduced him to all who stopped by their table. The question of the passers-by was inevitably the same, "Where's Brub?" It didn't occur to any of them that she had any interest in Dix.

Her answer was always the same. "He'll be along soon." And her introduction never varied. ". . . Dix Steele. Brub's best friend in England." Only once did she show any disturbance. She said it quietly, "I wonder what's keeping him."

At eight the bar was emptied of all but those whose goal was alcoholism. Her nervousness lay near the surface now. She pushed away from the table. "We might as well go to dinner. I'm sure he'll be here any moment."

He deliberately broke through the commonplaces then. "Don't apologize, Sylvia. I'm not missing Brub." His voice smiled at her. "I'm enjoying you—quite as much as I would Brub."

She laughed. And she said with a small moue, "I'm missing him. I haven't seen him since morning."

He mock sighed. "Still on your honeymoon."

"Definitely."

But he'd broken through; only a wedge perhaps, yet enough for a starter.

He waited until they were at the dinner table before he asked the question casually. "Is he on a big case?"

She looked at him. Her eyes were anxious. Then she looked away. "I don't know," she admitted. "He didn't say. Only he'd been delayed."

She hadn't seen the evening paper. He could have told her, but he didn't. Let Brub tell her. What she feared.

He saw Brub at that moment crossing the room. Brub looked worn. He put on a smile in answer to greetings as he passed the various tables, but it was a thin smile. It slipped away as quickly as it came.

Sylvia saw him almost as soon as Dix did. Anxiety sharpened her face. They were tacitly silent until Brub reached the table. He bent and kissed Sylvia. "Sorry I'm so late, darling." He didn't smile at them; he didn't need to pretend with his wife and best friend. He put out his hand to Dix, "Glad you could join us," then he sat down, dog-tiredness in every muscle. His suit was dog-tired too, and his linen showed the wilt of the day. His dark hair was crumpled. "I didn't have time to change." He smiled at Sylvia. "You can pretend I'm your chauffeur."

The waiter, a young colored man, whiter of skin than the beach-brown guests, was unobtrusive at the table.

Brub looked up. "Hello, Malcolm. Do you suppose you could get me a double Scotch from the bar before you start my dinner? I've just come from work, and I need it."

"I'm sure I can, Mr. Nicolai," Malcolm smiled. He went away.

Sylvia's hand covered Brub's on the table. "Hard day, darling?" She'd started casual, but she couldn't keep it up. Something about the set of Brub's mouth released her fear in a little gust. "It wasn't another—"

Brub's mouth was tight; his voice deliberately matter of fact. "Yes, another one."

"Brub!" She whispered it.

He began to light a cigarette; the flame wavered slightly. Dix watched the two with the proper attentiveness and the proper curiosity. When neither spoke, he let his curiosity become audible. "What's it all about?"

"Another woman killed . . . the same way."

Sylvia's hands were clenched.

Malcolm brought the drink.

"Thanks," Brub said, and saw Dix. "I'm sorry, chum. How about you?"

"The same," he grinned. He didn't want it for himself; an extra for Brub. To relax Brub. He began on his shrimp cocktail. "Are you assigned to the case?"

"Everyone in the department is on it," Brub said. He drank again, and he grimaced. "No, it's not my case, Dix. They don't put juniors on big stuff." He turned to Sylvia. "The commissioner called in the whole department. We've been with him since five, since I called you. Even hizzoner the mayor sat in." His mouth tightened. "We've got to stop it."

"Yes," Sylvia said. Her eyes were frightened; the color under her tan was gone. It was as if she had personal fright, as if the horror were close to her.

Dix said, "Someone important who was killed?" Malcolm set down the highball. "Thanks."

"No." Brub was halfway through his drink. "It's never anyone important." Again he realized he was talking to someone, not thinking aloud. "I forgot. You wouldn't know about it. Being a visitor." He could speak about it calmly; it seemed to relax him as much as a highball would. "The first one was about six months ago. March to be exact."

"March sixteenth," Sylvia said. "The night before the St. Patrick's party."

"We didn't know it was only the first then. It was a girl down on Skid Row. She was a nice enough kid for the life she lived, I guess. Danced in a bump-and-grind house down there. We found her in an alley. Strangled." He picked up his glass, emptied it. "No clues. Nothing. We wrote that one off as the neighborhood, even though we didn't get any leads. You usually can on Skid Row. The next one was in April." His hand reached for his empty glass.

Dix shoved his across. "Take mine. The shrimp are too good to dilute. Try them, Sylvia."

"Yes, don't wait for me," Brub said.

Sylvia picked up her fork, but she didn't do anything with it. Just held it loosely, her eyes on Brub's face.

He took a drink before continuing. "In April. We found her in Westlake Park. There wasn't any reason for it. She was a nice normal girl, young, attractive. She'd been to a movie with a couple of girlfriends. She lived in the Wilshire district, blocks from the park. No clues. She'd been killed the same way." He looked at Dix angrily. "There wasn't any reason for her to be killed. There's been no reason for any of them." Again he drank.

"There've been others?"

"Last night was the sixth," Brub said heavily. "One a month. Since March."

"Except last month," Sylvia said quickly. "There was none in August."

Brub continued, "No motive. No connection between any of them. Never the same neighborhood."

"Last night's—" Sylvia's voice was hushed, as if she dreaded the question.

Brub said, "A new neighborhood. Beverly Glen Canyon—up where it's country. She wasn't found until late this morning. She was lying in the brush at the side of the road." Anger clanged in his voice again. "It's like hunting a needle in a haystack. Los Angeles is too big—too sprawling. You can't patrol every street every night, all night. He's safe. A maniac walking the streets, looking just as normal as you or me, more normal probably."

"You'll get him," Sylvia said, pushing conviction into her wish.

"We'll get him." Brub believed it. "But how many women will be murdered first?" He tipped up the glass.

"You'd better eat, dear," Sylvia said. She forced herself to start eating.

"Yeah." Brub began spearing the shrimp, eating hurriedly, not tasting the food. "Take this girl last night. A nice girl like the others—except perhaps the first was a different cut. This one was a stenographer. Worked downtown. Lived in Hollywood. She'd been playing bridge with friends in Beverly. On South Camden. Just four girls. They played once a week, rotating the meeting place. They always quit early. None of them wanted to be out late, alone that way. Last night they stopped around eleven. The three left together, walked up to Wilshire together. The other two lived downtown farther. They took the Wilshire bus. Mildred was taking the Hollywoodland bus. Her name was Mildred Atkinson. She was still waiting when the girls' bus came along. She waved good-bye to them. No one saw her after that."

Sylvia had stopped eating. "It's horrible," she said.

"Yes, it's horrible," Brub agreed. "There's no reason for the pattern. If we could just get at what's behind it."

Dix put on a thoughtful frown. "Have you no leads at all?"

"Not much," Brub said. "There are no clues; there never are—no fingerprints or footprints. God, how we'd like just one fingerprint!" He returned to monotone. "We've double-checked all the known sex offenders."

"It's a sex crime?" Dix interrupted.

Brub nodded. "That's a part of it."

Sylvia's shiver was slight.

He continued, "We know one thing, of course. He works from a car."

Malcolm brought the chowder.

"How do you know that?" Dix asked.

"He has to. Take last night, for instance. The place is inaccessible without a car."

Dix scowled. "Can't you check tire prints?"

"We can't check every car in L.A.," Brub said helplessly. "It's the same as footprints. We can't check every pair of shoes in L.A."

"I understand that," Dix nodded. "Excellent chowder." But they'd have the tire tracks in plaster. If you could get them off concrete.

"We have an excellent chef at the club," Sylvia said. She had no appetite. Her soup was barely tasted when Malcolm brought the abalone steaks.

Dix began on his with relish. "What you know then is that there is a man and he has a car—"

"Yes. In the fourth case, he was seen."

Dix's eyebrows lifted. He held his fork in midair. "You mean you have a description?"

Brub sighed. "The fourth girl was seen leaving a movie with a man. As for description, hell!" He gestured. "The guy who noticed them, a tailor waiting for a street car, was half a block away. All he knew was the man was kind of young and sort of tall and normal looking. Only one head and no fangs!"

Dix smiled slightly. "Maybe he saw two other people."

"He saw them all right. But he was so busy looking at the girl's red suit, he didn't notice the man."

"No one else has ever seen him?"

"If they have, they've taken a vow of silence. You'd think he—"

34

Sylvia broke in, "Brub, let's talk about something else. Please, Brub. We asked Dix to a party, not a postmortem."

"Okay, sweetheart." He patted her hand. "I'm sorry. Sorry, Dix. How about another drink? Malcolm!"

Dix smiled. "I'll have another with you." He hid his annoyance. Just like a woman, interfering, imposing her whims on the party.

"Who's here tonight?" Brub edged his chair to look around. He lifted his hand to the group at the next table. "Hi, there."

Dix lit a cigarette and also surveyed the room. Nice people, healthy and wealthy. Normal as you and me. Normal as Sylvia when she didn't have the megrims. But you didn't know what was beneath beach-tanned faces and simple expensive clothes. You didn't ever know about thoughts. They were easily hidden. You didn't have to give away what you were thinking. No one exchanging pleasantries now with Brub would know that the man's mind was raw with murder. No one watching Sylvia replacing her lip rouge, smiling over the mirror of her bleached wooden compact, would know that fear was raveling her nerves. Even he, permitted as friend to know that there was fear in her veins, didn't know whether the fear was for Brub's safety or her own. Or an atavistic fear of reasonless death.

The color under her sunbrown had returned as she did the little normal things of lipstick, cigarette. He could make it recede so easily, a word, or one more question on the subject. He could make her heart stop beating as easily. With a simple statement. His lips smiled. And his eyes again turned to the room. Away from temptation.

It was then that he saw her, the little brown girl. It almost shocked him for a moment. She didn't belong here; she belonged out in the dark. She wasn't a brown girl tonight, save for her healthy beach color. She was in starchy white, an evening dress, cut low on her brown back, flaring to her white sandals. She had a young, laughing face, short brown curly hair. She was at the table directly across the floor. He should have seen her earlier. He had, he realized, but only the brown back and white piqué dress. She'd shifted her chair as Brub had, bringing her face to the room.

He took a long draw on his cigarette before he asked, deliberately casual, "Who's the girl over there?"

Brub turned back to their table. "Which one?"

Sylvia followed Dix's gesture.

"Over there. In white."

Brub peered. "Oh, that one. I've seen her—who is she, Sylvia?"

Sylvia had placed the girl. "Betsy Banning. You know, Brub. The Bannings bought the Henry house up the beach." Sylvia said to Dix, "I've met her, but I don't really know her." She smiled, "Or I'd introduce you."

Dix laughed. "Don't start matchmaking. I'm happy. She looked familiar, that was all. Is she in pictures?"

"No," Sylvia answered. "She's at the university, I believe." She smiled. "She doesn't need the pictures; the Bannings are Texas oil, floating in it. Otis Banning, her father, is the bald one. They say he has seven million in a little black box. No doubt an exaggeration."

Brub said, "Sylvia ought to be the detective in the family. She knows everything about everybody."

"Otis and I share the same dentist, darling."

"She's a cute kid." Brub was again looking across at the girl.

"You're married now," Dix reminded him.

"To me," Sylvia added sweetly. "I may not be a cute kid, but I'm nice."

They exchanged that happy intimate look. Then Brub turned his eyes again to the Banning girl. "You're right, though. She does look familiar." He was scenting her, the way a detective would, narrowed eyes, his brows pulled slightly together, his nose keen.

"Come on home," Dix laughed.

Brub's head snapped to Dix quickly. His dark eyes were lighted. "That's it! You know who she looks like? Brucie!"

The name was spoken before he could warn Brub not to speak it. He'd known in that split second of Brub's remembering, in the second before the name. It was said, and for the moment he could see nothing, only the red blur before his eyes and the dread roaring of sound in his ears. He didn't know his knuckles were white knobs gripping the table, his cigarette mashed between his fingers. The moment passed, and he was in control of himself again. He let the cigarette brush to the floor. In another moment he could speak.

Sylvia spoke first. "And who is Brucie, darling?"

"A girl we knew in England. She was a Red Cross worker when we were stationed near Dover. Scotch—that's where the Bruce, Brucie, came from. Cute as a button."

Brub had noticed nothing. But he wasn't sure about Sylvia. Behind her civilized attention, her humor, her casualness, he wasn't certain. Something was there behind the curtain of her eyes, something in the way she looked at Dix, a look behind the look. She might have been watching him at that wrong moment.

Dix said, "She was, all of that." His voice wasn't thick; it was as casual as Sylvia's.

"Wonder what ever happened to her? She was sure a cute kid. You kind of went for her, didn't you, Dix?"

Dix laughed, a normal laugh. "You kind of liked her yourself, didn't you?"

"Brub!" Sylvia's eyes opened, wide surprise. She was pretending. She was too levelheaded, too secure to care.

"You bet I liked her. I guess every man in the platoon sort of liked Brucie. But you needn't worry, honey. No one had a chance with old lady-killer Steele present."

Dix was very careful lighting his cigarette. Because Sylvia was watching him. With the look behind the look.

"You ever hear from her, Dix?"

He shook his head. He was surprised at how easy it was to talk. "No, Brub, I never did."

"Out of sight, out of mind. That's the great Steele. Don't ever fall for a guy like that, Sylvia." Brub began on his neglected ice cream.

"No, darling," Sylvia murmured. She wasn't looking at him, yet Dix had a feeling she was seeing him. And probing him with her mind.

"If I'd had a girl like Sylvia," he began, and he realized there was some honesty in the play, "I wouldn't have looked at anyone else. I wouldn't have been like you, ogling all those U.S.O. legs."

"I'm learning things." Sylvia nodded a severe head. "Go on, Dix, tell me more."

He invented lazily, but his mind wasn't there. It was remembering Brucie, and the ache in him was the ache of a wound torn open. His face covered his mind, as his voice covered the pain crying from his throat. "Remember the redhead contortionist?" and he remembered the redhead in the patio this afternoon. With a woman like that, he might be able to forget. Nothing else brought forgetfulness, only for a brief time. Another section of his mind moved as the brown girl stood up from her table with her young crew-cut escort. The look of Brucie, not the face, the swagger of her shoulders, the echo of laughter. Perhaps married to seven million dollars, you could forget. You could have fast cars, fast boats, a good plane to climb up there into the vastness of eternity. Brub and Sylvia were happy. Marriage could be happy.

He realized there was music when the brown girl and her partner began to dance. He should ask Sylvia to dance. But he didn't want to. He wanted to get out of here, to go home. He couldn't leave abruptly, not two nights in a row. However, he didn't think the Nicolais would stay much longer; off guard their faces returned to somberness. He could nudge them. He said abruptly, "You're tired, Brub."

Brub nodded, "Yeah. But I've got to go back to work."

"No, Brub," Sylvia cried.

"I shouldn't have left when I did."

"You're worn out now. You can't, darling. It's an hour's drive downtown—"

He interrupted, "I don't have to go downtown, Sylvia. To the Beverly Hills station is all. That isn't fifteen minutes. Why don't you keep Dix—"

Sylvia shook her head.

Dix said, "I ought to get back to work myself. So don't be polite."

Sylvia said, "I couldn't stay. You understand."

He gave her an appreciative smile. "I understand."

"It's been a punk evening for you, Dix," Brub was apologetic. "We'll make it up to you."

They almost hurried from the dining room into the lounge. As if, once it had been admitted, all three could make up with haste for the spent time. Sylvia said, "I'll get my coat." She hesitated, "You are on the case, Brub?"

He admitted ruefully, "Just a little bit, honey."

She didn't say anything, simply turned and went to the cloakroom. Brub watched her go.

"Why is she afraid?" Dix asked.

Brub started, "Wha—" He realized Dix's question. "I guess it's pretty much my fault. Ever since this thing started, I've been afraid for her. She's lived in the canyon all her life. She never had any fear, wandered all over it, any time of day. But the canyon at night, the way the fogs come in—it's a place for *him*." His face was again angry, helplessly angry. "I've scared her. She's alone so much. I never know what hours I have to keep. We have good neighbors—a couple of our best friends are right across the road.

But you know our street. It's dark and lonely, and the way our house is set up there—" He broke off. "I'm the one who's scared; I've infected her. And I can't help it. I can't pretend, until we've caught him—"

Sylvia was coming into the hall. She looked herself again, tall and lovely and unruffled, her gilt hair smooth, her movements unhurried.

Brub said under his breath, "If we could only find the why of the pattern—" He didn't finish because she was there, and the three were moving out of the club into the sea-fresh darkness. The swish of the breakers was liquid against the night.

"I could take Sylvia—" Dix began.

"No, I'll run her home, get her settled. Unless you'd like to sit with her until I—"

"Dix has to work," Sylvia said. "And I'm tired." She put out her hand. "Another time we'll do better, Dix."

"We certainly will," Brub vowed.

He watched Brub wheel the car out of the drive. In a hurry, hurried to get back to the Beverly Hills police station. He would take Sylvia into the house, make sure there was no shadowy stranger lurking. They would cling together for a moment, fear in both of them. The woman fearing to have her man sniffing the spoor of a murderer, fearing lest he catch up with evil. Fearing less for herself; only the unease she must feel, infected by Brub's fear for her. Brub fearing for her because she was a woman, because she was his woman, and women were being stalked in the night. Fearing, he would yet leave her, and quickly, because he was a hunter and this was a big hunt. For wild game.

Dix circled back to his car, Terriss's car. The plain black coupe. He warmed the engine. It was a good car, and he kept it functioning smoothly. He released the brake. Fifteen minutes at the outside and Brub would be gone. He could go there then; she'd let him in. Brub's friend. He could have an excuse, Brub could have infected him too with the fear. She'd be glad to see him. He could coax her into driving up to Malibu. For a drink. For fresh air. She wouldn't be afraid—at first.

He slide the car to the gates. Left lay the canyon. Left lay Malibu. Right was the California Incline. Right was Wilshire, the road back to town. She was Brub's wife. Brub was his friend. Brub, the hunter.

He was very tired. He hadn't had much sleep last night. He turned to the right.

## 2

THE morning paper had columns on the case. Having been scooped by the afternoon papers on the original story, this sheet at least was making up its loss by intensive research. It had pictures of the girl, Mildred, of her family, of the apartment house where she'd played bridge, of the lonely spot in Beverly Glen Canyon where her body was found.

Her name was Mildred Atkinson, and she had led a very stupid life. Grade school, high school—Hollywood High, but she was no beauty queen—business college, and a job in an insurance office. She was twenty-six years old and she was a good girl, her parents sobbed. She played bridge with girlfriends, and she once taught a Sunday-school class. She didn't have any particular gentleman friend; she went out with several. Not often, you could bet. The only exciting thing that had ever happened to her was to be raped and murdered. Even then she'd only been subbing for someone else.

The sleuths had found that she and the man had had a cup of coffee about midnight in a near drive-in. The couple had been served inside, not in a car. She'd been standing there alone, waiting for a bus. Her girlfriends had waved good-bye to her. The man had seen her standing there alone, a little nervous. He'd said, "Busses don't run often at night," as if he too were waiting. She hadn't wanted to talk; she'd been brought up not to talk to strange men. "Mildred was a good girl," the parents sobbed. She'd never let a man pick her up, her girlfriends chorused, but they wondered how much they hadn't known about Mildred. "Not unless she knew him." The cops were scouring the town now, talking to every man Mildred had known. They'd be thorough; they'd check every man who'd passed through that insurance office. Believing they had a lead at last on a man apparently as normal as you or I, who tracked women at night. The lead editorial called him Jack the Ripper and demanded more and better police protection. The editorial—it was a non-administration paper—sneered politics and got in some snide cracks about the mayor.

She didn't want to talk, but he was a decent-looking young fellow waiting for a bus. And the mist grew cold on the lonely corner. When he knew she was ripe for the suggestion, he mentioned coffee at the drive-in up at the corner of Linden Drive. The pert carhop remembered Mildred when she saw the picture in the paper. She'd been carrying out a tray when they entered. Remembered possibly because by then Mildred was pleased at having coffee with a good-looking young fellow. She'd preened a little.

The carhop told the other girls, "That's her"; the boss heard the gabble, and he called the Beverly Hills police. The carhop couldn't describe the man, sort of tall, nice-looking in a tan suit. She was sure he couldn't be the strangler; he wasn't that kind of a man at all. She would always be sure that what happened to Mildred happened after she left her drive-in escort.

He read every line of every story in the morning paper. He felt good today after last night's sleep. It was a wonderful summer day. He stretched out in bed lazily, and he thought about the redhead. She would be poison, but it wouldn't hurt to think about her. He couldn't get mixed up with a woman, with a damn snooping dame. But God, she'd be worth knowing. It had been so long a time since he'd had a woman to hold to. He hadn't wanted one.

He didn't want one now; it was hangover from seeing Sylvia and Brub looking at each other. Maybe the crazy thought that had flickered in his mind about the little brown girl and her seven million dollars. It would be a good day to lie on the beach at Santa Monica. In front of Betsy Banning's house at the foot of the California Incline. He might even find out which house was Banning's.

He stretched off the bed. If he were going to sun on the beach, it might be smart to call Brub. Brub shouldn't be working on Sunday. He should be beaching. Talking about the case. New developments. He smiled. It was neat to have a source of information on a case.

A quick shot of thought jabbed him. The tires. They were good tires, no patches, no distinguishing marks. Only somewhere in the back of his mind, he remembered that all tires had distinguishing marks, like fingerprints. Could they get a cast of tire marks from dry concrete? He doubted it. As he had doubted it last night. But he should make sure.

Certain gambles were legitimate. Like appearing in a lighted place with Mildred. Gambling on the muddled memory of waitresses and countermen who served hundreds of average-looking men and women every day, every night. Risks were spice. Stunt flying. As long as you used them like spice, sparingly; like stunts, planning them with precision, carrying them out boldly.

He fingered his lip. He could grow a mustache. No reason why he should. He didn't like lip brushes. He looked like a thousand other men. He'd never been in that drive-in before. He never intended to go in it again. Risks he took; mistakes he didn't make.

It would be better to call up the Nicolais. He could find out where the Bannings lived easily enough. If he was going to marry the girl, he'd have to find out where she lived. Too bad she wasn't a pal of Sylvia's. That would make it easy. He lifted the phone, dialed the Santa Monica number. There was no answer, only metallic ringing. Too late; they'd probably already gone to the beach. It was past one o'clock.

He wasn't too disappointed. He dressed leisurely, tan gabardine slacks, a white T-shirt. He left the house by the front door. On the balcony were open doors, musical radios, laughter. If she lived in Virginibus Arms—he was certain she did; she hadn't walked like a visitor—he'd run into her again. Plenty of time. Mel Terriss wouldn't be back for a long time.

He walked around the block to the garage, opened the noiseless doors. Before taking out the car, he circled it, kicking the tires. They were in good shape, not worn, good solid tires. He didn't need new ones; there was no reason to go to that expense. Brub had said it: the police couldn't check every pair of tires in L.A.

He backed out and swung over to Wilshire, turned west. The road to the beach. About three million other drivers had the same idea on this blue-sky, golden-warm day in late September. He took the San Vicente cutoff, as he turned noting the eucalyptus grove with one small corner of his mind. Not exactly secluded, yet late enough. . . . At Fourth Street in Santa Monica he right-turned again, descending into the canyon. The sign pointed this as an alternate road to the beach. He was prospecting. This descent would be pretty well deserted at night. But no underbrush except fenced. He dropped into the canyon and found Mesa Road. He didn't expect to find the Nicolais at home, but it was worth a try.

It was well worth it; the door was open. Through the screen he could see into the hallway. He pushed the bell, pleased with himself, relaxed, comfortable. It was Sylvia who answered, and she was surprised to see him. By her startled look, you'd think he was someone unexpectedly returned from Limbo.

"Hello," he said easily. "Anyone home?"

"Dix—" She unhooked the screen, pushing it open. "I didn't recognize you at first. The sun behind you." She had an open white beach robe over brief white shorts and a white cleft brassiere. Her skin was deep tan, and her gilt hair was loose about her shoulders. Without the cool poise, she seemed much younger. She was flustered. "Excuse the way I look." Her feet were bare and dappled with sand. "We've just come up from the beach, and Brub beat me to the shower. I didn't expect you. Some friends were coming over—"

He cut her off, "I'm a friend too."

She colored. "Of course, you are. I mean, old friends." She sighed. "I'm making it worse. Go on in and get comfortable. Help yourself to a drink. I'll tell Brub." She went quickly, too quickly.

Maybe his open admiration embarrassed her. He didn't understand Sylvia. She was too many women. He settled himself on the living-room couch. Friends coming in. He wouldn't stay on. He'd have a dinner date.

Brub wasn't long. His face lighted when he saw Dix; it had been heavy at the doorway. "Where's that drink? Sylvia said you were mixing them."

"What am I, the bartender?" Dix lounged off the couch. "Name it."

"No," Brub waved him down. "I'll do it. I'm handy."

He felt too good to bother with a drink. "I don't care. Whatever you're having."

"Then you'll settle for Scotch and splash," Brub said from behind the bar. "That's the only English I learned in the service. We'll have it with ice though." He filled the glasses. "What you been doing all day?"

"Working," Dix answered. "Tried to reach you earlier. I wanted to play hookey on the beach." He took the glass. "Thanks. I thought you were probably on the job."

Brub frowned a little. "I worked this morning." He pushed away the frown. "Spent the afternoon on the beach."

Dix tasted his highball. "How's the case coming?" He had just the right casual curiosity in his voice. It pleased him.

The frown returned to Brub's forehead. "It's not. Right where it was."

Dix's foot edged the paper on the floor. "But you found someone who saw her with the man."

"Yeah." Brub's voice was flat. "Maybe if he'd walk in again, that carhop would remember him." He was disgusted. "She's looked through the files of every known offender, and she can't even describe the guy anymore. She thinks he was this and maybe he was that. She doesn't even know the color of his eyes."

"That's too bad." Dix was gravely sympathetic. "No one else noticed the couple?"

"If they did, they've got stage fright. No one else has volunteered any information. And it was a crowded time at the drive-in. The after-movie crowd. Somebody else must have seen them."

"Yeah," Dix said. "Though you can see people without noticing them." He enlarged on it as if he'd never thought of it before. "How many times in a restaurant do you notice people around you? You don't pay any attention to them when they come or when they go. At least I don't."

"That's it," Brub agreed. He went on, "There's one thing we do know."

Dix lifted his eyes with renewed interest.

"We know he was in Beverly Hills on Friday night." Brub was sardonic. "But whether he was in the neighborhood for an evening's pleasure"—he bit his lip—"or whether he lives there, we don't know. He can't live all over Southern California. He's probably never operated in his own neighborhood; he'd be too cagey for that."

Sylvia came in on the end of his sentence. "Brub, you're not talking the case again. I can't take it." She was as different from the girl who'd opened the screen door as from the frightened woman of last night. She looked glowing, slim as a birch, in pale gray slacks, a brilliant green sweater. Her damp hair was braided on top of her head. "That's all I've heard this afternoon. Everyone on the beach hounding Brub for details. Do I get a drink, darling?"

"You do. Same as us?" Brub went to the bar again.

"Please, darling." Sylvia dumped ashtrays with zeal. "Why people are so damn morbid," she returned to the subject with emphasis. She'd set up a hearty defense mechanism to battle her fears.

Dix remonstrated, "I don't know that it's exactly morbidity. Isn't it rather self-importance?" He grinned. "It isn't everyone who can get a firsthand account from the detective in the case."

Brub said, "Yeah, Junior G-Man tells all. He don't know nothing, but he gotta say something." He swizzled the soda.

Dix smiled into his drink. "I'm different. I have a personal interest in the case." He let his eyes lift lazily as he spoke. Sylvia had frozen where she stood, her eyes alone moving, her eyes slewing swiftly to his face as if he'd suddenly revealed himself as the strangler. Brub went on swizzling.

"You see, I'm writing a detective novel," Dix added.

Sylvia moved then, setting down the ashtray she held. It made a small clack on the glass-topped end table.

Brub brought her the highball. "Here you are, skipper." He sat down, hanging his feet over the arm of the green chair. "So that's what you're writing. Who you stealing from, Chandler or Hammett or Gardner?"

"Little of each," Dix agreed. "With a touch of Queen and Carr."

"It should be a best seller if you combine all those," Sylvia said. She sat opposite Brub.

"Can't miss," Dix admitted. "But for God's sake don't tell Uncle Fergus what I'm doing. He thinks I'm writing literature."

"I don't know Uncle Fergus," Sylvia murmured.

"You wouldn't like him. He's vehemently conservative. He hasn't relaxed since Hoover left Washington," he added cheerfully. "He won't mind what I've written when the royalties roll in. He won't read it anyway." She tried to stymie him on his questioning; he'd fixed that. He said, "Now you take that business about tire tracks that Brub mentioned last night. Instead of beating my brains out at the library, all I have to do is ask him. It's a good touch for a story. Makes you sound like an expert." He lifted his glass. "Do they really make plaster casts of tracks, Brub?"

"They try," Brub said gloomily. "But it takes cooperation. For good ones, you need skid marks or mud or virgin territory. No chance this time. There weren't more than several hundred tracks superimposed on that particular stretch. Not worth lifting them."

"But you lifted them, didn't you?" Dix wondered. "The thoroughness of the police—"

"Sure," Brub grunted. "Thorough as hell. Maybe next time—" He broke off. Sylvia had gone tense. "There mustn't be a next time," he said heatedly. "Only now—"

Dix said seriously, "Let's skip it, Brub. With you working on it, feeling the way you do, you'll get him." Sylvia's eyes were grateful. "I'll take a refill, and I'll tell you about the redhead at my apartment. You still like redheads?"

Sylvia's gratefulness was gay. "He'd better not."

"Who is she?" Brub played up, taking Dix's glass and his own. But it was an effort; he was pulling by his bootstraps.

"Well, I haven't met her yet," Dix laughed. "But I'm working on it." He knew better than to be talking about a woman publicly; he knew he shouldn't even think about her. "As soon as I find which apartment is hers, I'm going to get a job reading the light meter or delivering laundry. She's the sweetest built job I've seen in Hollywood."

"You better have me look her over before you make any commitments," Brub said. "Don't forget that blonde in London. Whew!"

"How was I to know her husband was a brass hat? With brass knuckles." He wanted the second drink less than the first but it tasted good.

"You'd better let me look her over," Sylvia suggested. "I don't trust Brub's taste. He just looks at the envelope. Now, I'm a psychologist. I find out what's inside."

"You're both invited. As soon as I read the meter."

"That shouldn't take you long," Brub railed. "Unless you're getting old." He squinted his eyes. "You don't show much wear."

Voices clacked on the porch.

"That'll be Maude and Cary," Sylvia said. She called, "Come on in."

They were about what Dix had expected. A cute, babbling brunette, big-eyed, hips too wide for her salmon slacks. A nice, empty-looking guy in gabardine slacks and a sports shirt. The Jepsons. Maude liked Dix. She baby-eyed him while she headed for the couch. He'd finish the drink and get out.

She said, "You're the ace, aren't you? I've heard all about you." There was a Texas drawl in her voice. She put a cigarette in her mouth and waited for him to light it. She smelled of perfume and liquor. "Make mine weak, Brub. We had one before leaving." She turned back to Dix. "You were in England with Brub." She babbled at Dix until Brub put the drink in her hand. She started on Brub then; it was inevitable what she would say.

"Have you caught that man yet, Brub? I tell you I'm so scared I don't know what to do. I won't let Cary leave me alone for a minute. I tell him—"

She ought to be scared. It would be a pleasure to throttle her.

"Anything new?" Cary put in.

"No," Brub said.

Sylvia said firmly, "We're not going to talk about it tonight."

Maude ignored her. "Why can't the police catch him?" She was highly indignant. "Nobody's safe with him running around loose." She whispered in sepulchre tones, "The strangler." She shivered closer to Dix. She was having a swell time.

Sylvia took a preparatory breath, but Maude raced on, "How are we supposed to know who he is? He could be anybody. I tell Cary maybe he's our grocery man or the bus driver or those dreadful beach athletes. We don't know. Even the police don't know. You'd think they could find out."

Sylvia said desperately, "For God's sake, Maude. Don't you think they're trying?"

"I don't know." Maude tossed her head. "Maybe it's one of their own men. Well, it could be," she insisted to the rejection on the faces of the others. "How do we know? It's simply silly to think that this nice-looking fellow she had coffee with is the one. How did he get her into Beverly Glen Canyon?" she demanded. "Did they walk?"

Cary grunted, "He had a car, of course, Maude."

"Ah." She pounced on it. "But he didn't have a car. They went into the drive-in for coffee." She cocked her triumph at all of them. Her husband looked tired of it all, but a thin layer of fear came over Sylvia's doubt.

Brub was scowling. He said, "That's just one of the things we're trying to find out, Maude. He must have had a car."

"I don't get it," Dix admitted.

"Our effete Easterner." Brub seized the diversion. "Dix is from New Jersey," he explained, and turned to Dix again. "No one goes into a drive-in for a cup of coffee. Not if he has a car to sit outside in."

"But I've seen people in the drive-ins," Dix argued.

"Kids without a car. Or folks who've walked to the neighborhood movie. Or someone who's after a full meal, something he doesn't want to balance on a tray. But not for a shake or a cup of coffee. That's the point of a drive-in. You don't have to get out of your car."

"If you don't have a car, then you have to sit inside." Maude wagged her head. "He couldn't have had a car. Because," she took a deep breath, "because if he was the strangler and had a car, he never would have taken her inside where people could identify him. That man didn't have a car. But the one who killed her did have a car, or she wouldn't have been found up Beverly Glen." Her triumph skittered joyfully. "There has to be another man with a car."

Dix narrowed his eyes, as if with the others he was pondering her conviction.

Sylvia broke the pause. "You think then that there was a second man, an accomplice." She looked quickly at Brub.

Brub shook his head. "He works alone." There was certainty in him.

Dix didn't jump on the statement. He asked simply, "How do you know that?"

"His kind of killer always works alone. He can't risk an accomplice."

Cary said, "He's insane, of course."

Dix turned his glass in his hand. Cary Jepson was a clod. He wouldn't be married to a stupid little talking machine if he had any spirit. The obvious reach of his imagination was, "He's insane, of course." It would never occur to him that any reason other than insanity could make a man a killer. That's what all the dolts around town would be parroting: *he's insane of course he's insane of course.* It took imagination to think of a man, sane as you or I, who killed. He hid against his highball glass the smile forming on his lips.

Brub was explaining, "—but doubtless he's a loony only in that respect. Otherwise he's probably an everyday citizen. Going about his business like any of us. Looking normal, acting normal until that urge comes on him."

"About once a month," Maude said, goggle-eyed, and then she screamed, "Oh."

Dix moved slightly away to look down at her. There was nothing wrong; she was just acting up. Sylvia didn't like it. Sylvia's face was granite. Dix didn't like it either; he was getting out of here.

Brub said, "Just don't be out alone at night, Maude, and you needn't worry." He added, almost to himself, "We'll get him. He'll make a mistake yet." His mouth was grim.

"Suppose he doesn't," Maude wailed. She savored it, "Suppose it goes on and on—"

"Maude!" her husband complained wearily. "She keeps raving like that—"

Sylvia said definitely, "She isn't going to rave here. That's all, Maude. It's a truce—no more talk about crime tonight." She put on a bright smile. "Where will we eat? Ted's for steak? Carl's for shrimp? Jack's for chowder?"

He could leave now. Dix glanced at his watch and stood upright fast. "Why didn't someone tell me? I've a dinner date in Hollywood at seven. I've got to beat it."

Maude pushed out her spoiled underlip. "Break it."

"With a redhead?" Brub grinned.

Dix grinned back. "Not yet. I'll keep you informed. Thanks, Sylvia. Ring me, Brub. We'll have lunch." He nodded good-bye to the Jepsons, not saying it was a pleasure to meet them; it hadn't been.

He took a deep breath outside to expel the odor of Maude from his lungs. He'd like to meet her on a dark corner. It would be a service to humanity.

He drove the beach road to the Incline, casually glancing towards the three houses there. The traffic was still fairly heavy. On Wilshire it became irritating; at Sepulveda's intersection, it was a slow-moving mass. Enough to make anyone's nerves short. He left-turned at Westwood Boulevard, cutting sharp, just missing a right-turning car. He saw the motorcycle cop as the brakes of the other car screamed. But the cop didn't come after him.

He drove slowly up through the university gates and onto Sunset. Only one stop sign, at Beverly Glen. Sunset seemed deserted after Wilshire. He picked up speed. The light was against him at the intersection. He glanced casually at the Bel-Air gates; the road north jogged here, dividing into Bel-Air Road and, just beyond, Beverly Glen.

His hands tightened on the wheel. Cops again. Not on cycles; in a prowl car. Parked there watching the cars. He slid with the change to Go, not gathering speed until he had rounded the corner of the twisting woodland Sunset stretch. The rearview mirror showed no car following. His hands relaxed, and he wanted to laugh. Out loud, noisy.

The cops were as unimaginative as that Jepson. Could they actually believe the killer would return to the scene of the crime? He did laugh, and loud. He could see them sitting there all day, waiting for a loony to drive up the canyon. Fools.

He cut south at Rodeo, swinging back to Wilshire. He had nothing to do with himself, and tonight he didn't want to be alone. The routine dullness of his nights, eat alone, go to a movie, go home—or, skip the movie, go home and read, write a little sometimes. The end, the same. Take some dope to sleep. Unless he could sleep the sleep of exhaustion. That wasn't often.

A man couldn't live alone; he needed friends. He needed a woman, a real woman. Like Brub and Sylvia. Like that stupid Cary had that stupid Maude. Better than being alone.

It wasn't often it hit him hard. It was the balmy night and the early dusk and the look of lamps through opened windows and the sound of music from radios in the lighted rooms. He'd eschewed human relationship for something stronger, something a hell of a lot better.

The car had followed its lead to the apartment; he hadn't intended to come back here yet. He parked at the curb; he'd have to go out to eat. Later.

He didn't have to give up normal living; that had been his one mistake. Brub and Sylvia proved it. He could be with them and be himself and not give away any secrets. His nerves were steady, his eyes level. It was time to gather friends again. Someone besides Brub and Sylvia. He couldn't be so constant at their home. They might start wondering. Sometimes Sylvia's eyes were disturbing, they were so wise. As if she could see under the covering of a man. Ridiculous, of course. You didn't ever have to give yourself away. Not if you were smart.

His spirits had jutted back up to a normal level. It wasn't often he got the dumps. His life was good, a slick apartment, a solid car; income without working for it, not half enough, but he could get by. Freedom, plenty of freedom. Nobody telling him what to do, nobody snooping.

He pulled the keys from the ignition and walked, tinkling them, the few paces to the court entrance. It was amusing to enter boldly, announcing his entrance with the metallic percussion. He didn't let into actual consciousness the thought that the redhead might be on her balcony.

The first time he'd seen the patio, he hadn't believed it. He hadn't been long enough in Southern California to believe it. It wasn't real; it was a stage set, a stagy stage set. In the center was the oblong blue pool. By day the pool was sky blue; it was tiled in that color, the water in it had to look that blue. By night it was moonlight blue. Two blue spotlights, one at either end of the balcony, made certain of that.

Dix had never seen anyone swimming in the pool by day or by night. He'd never seen anyone lounging in the bright, striped gliders or around the gaudy umbrella tables. The idea was good, the semitropical flowers spotted in the corners of the square prettied it up still more, the high oleander hedge was protection from

54

street eyes, but nobody used the patio. The people in the Spanish bungalows boxing the court on three sides and those upstairs off the Spanish-Colonial balcony weren't clubby. Dix hadn't laid eyes on a couple of them in the weeks he'd been here.

He was thinking about the artificial moonlight in the artificial patio when behind him the blare of a horn jabbed. Jangle of voices scraped across his nerves. Anger shook him; for a moment he was tempted to turn out of the court and raise hell. Instead he tightened his fists and walked to his door, the first bungalow on the left. He was only at the door when he heard the heels clicking across the flagstone patio. Before he turned, he was certain whom he would see.

She hadn't noticed him standing there by his door; she was hurrying. In the blue light her hair and her slacks and jacket were all blue, different depths of blue.

What he did was out of impulse, without thought. Thought would have rejected the idea. With long stride he quietly circled the pool. He was at the stairs almost as quickly as she. She was only on the third step when he spoke to her.

"I beg your pardon."

She wasn't startled, although she hadn't known he was there. She stood arrested in motion of ascent, her head turning without any haste until she could look back down at him. When she saw it was a man, the glint of dare touched her mouth, her eyes.

"Did you drop something?" he continued. He held one hand cupped before him.

She looked down at herself, at her purse, touched her blown hair. "Did I?" she puzzled.

Quickly, impudently, he thrust both hands in his pockets. He looked up boldly at her. "I don't know. I was hoping so."

Her eyes narrowed over him slowly, in the way they had last night. She liked the look of him. Her eyes lengthened, and she began to smile her lips. "Why?" she countered.

"I just lost my dinner date. I thought maybe you'd lost yours too."

She stopped smiling, and she froze up just a little, not much. His eyes didn't waver; they held on to hers until she smiled again. "Sorry."

"I'm your neighbor. One A." His head gestured. He didn't want her to think he was a stranger, trying for a pickup.

"Sorry," she repeated, and she moved up to the fourth step. "My dinner date will be here any minute, and I'm not dressed. I'm rushing."

"I'm sorry too," Dix said. He said it warmly, with all the charm he could summon, and only a touch of arrogance for diversion.

She broke in, "If I ever lose a dinner date, I'll let you know." She ran up the stairs lightly, not looking back at him.

He shrugged. He hadn't expected success, therefore he wasn't disappointed. He'd made the preliminary maneuver; the question now was of time. He was stimulated by merely talking with her; she was a lure, even with that ghostly blue light coating her face. He moved back to his own quarters. Hearing again the tap of her heels, he swung suddenly and looked up to the balcony. She was just entering her apartment, the darkened one, the third. He continued, content, to his bungalow. He'd made headway. He knew now where to find her.

# 3

HE DIDN'T have to hurry. As a matter of fact, he needn't leave the apartment. There were tins of food, crackers, some cheese and fruit, cold meat in the ice box. He could get comfortable. Cheese and beer were good enough for any man on the evening of a scorcher day. But he didn't want to get comfortable; he wanted something lively. Something amusing and stimulating and male.

He switched on the radio, found music, and fetched himself a cold beer from the kitchen. He was sprawled on the couch, half listening to the program, half thinking about the things he'd like to do tonight. If he had the money and the woman.

The slow beer was half gone when his front doorbell sounded. It startled him momentarily; his front bell was never rung. Slowly he got to his feet. He didn't delay moving to answer it. But he didn't hurry. He walked with caution.

The breath he took before setting his hand to the knob wasn't deliberate. Not until he flung open the door and heard the breath expelled did he realize he'd been holding it.

On the doorstep was the redhead. She said, "I've just lost a dinner date."

He tried not to sound too foolishly pleased. "Come in. Maybe you'll find him here."

"I hope not," she said dryly. She moved past him into the living room. She was eyeing it. It didn't look so good, the Sunday papers crushed on the couch, spilling over to the floor. The limp sofa cushions. The ashtrays dirty, the beer bottle standing on the rug. Yet even in disarray it was class. The gray-green walls might have been indigenous to Virginibus Arms, but the furniture was hand-picked by Terriss. All modern bleached wood and glass and chrome, upholstery in yellow and crimson and gray. Terriss had boasted of his decorating taste. It wasn't personal taste, it was money; with Terriss's money you were steered to taste. You couldn't go wrong.

Dix said, "Tillie doesn't come on Sundays."

"You should see my place." She slid down in the wing chair as if she belonged there. She was still wearing the slacks; the outfit wasn't shades of moonlight blue but pale yellow, the pullover deeper yellow; the jacket, loose over her shoulders, was white.

And her hair wasn't red, it was burnt sienna with shimmer of gold dusting it. She'd done over her hair and her face, but she hadn't taken time to change.

Dix held out the cigarette box to her. "What do you mean you hope not?"

She put the cigarette in her mouth, lifted her face, waited for the light. From the thin gold lighter, Mel's lighter. "Because I told him I had a lousy headache and was going to bed." She blew the plume of smoke directly up at Dix. "And that I was disconnecting the phone."

He laughed. She was bold as her rust-red mouth and her slanted eyes, sharp as her painted tapering nails. She was what he'd needed. She was what he wanted. "Drink?"

"No. I want dinner. I had enough cocktails before I came home." She moved her body in the chair. "Maybe that's why I'm here." Her eyes studied the room.

"Mind if I finish my beer?"

"Not at all."

He returned to the couch and picked up the bottle. He didn't bother to pick up the newspapers. The way the first section had fallen revealed half of Mildred's whey face. He rested his foot on the paper.

The redhead turned her eyes suddenly back to him. "This is Mel Terriss's apartment." It wasn't a question.

"Yes. He's in South America. He turned it over to me while he's away."

"Who are you?" she demanded.

He smiled slightly. "I'm Dix Steele." In turn demanded, "Who are you?"

She wasn't accustomed to being given her own treatment. She didn't know whether she liked it. She tossed back her autumn hair and waited, her eyes watching him. And then accepted his equality. "Laurel Gray."

He inclined his head. "How d'y'do." Exaggerated politeness. He switched to impudence. "Married?"

She bridled. Retort was on her tongue, but she withheld it, her eyes going over him again in that slow slant fashion. There was no wedding ring on her finger; there was a lump of twisted gold, channeled with rubies and diamonds. A glittering bauble, the kind that cost fat money, the kind you looked at in jewelers' windows on Beverly Drive. You looked through the thick plate glass of the windows and wondered about those jeweled hunks. Wondered how a man could get his hands on the kind of dough it took to touch.

Somebody had put it on her finger. But there wasn't a wedding ring beside it.

She answered coolly, "It's none of your business, son, but since you asked, not now." She lifted her chin, and he knew what she was about to say. He didn't want it said; he fended it away quickly.

"You were a friend of Mel Terriss?" The ring might have come from Terriss.

"Not much." She stubbed her cigarette into the ashtray. "Dropped in on a couple of his parties." She eyed him. "You a friend of Mel's?"

She was like all women, curious about your private life. He laughed at her; she'd find out only as much as he wished. "An old friend," he laughed. "Prewar. Princeton." Princeton meant money and social position to her, calculation came that quickly under her skin. She was greedy and callous and a bitch, but she was fire, and a man needed fire. "I'm from New York," he threw in carelessly. It sounded better than New Jersey.

"So you looked up old friend Mel when you came to the coast," her voice mocked.

"What do you think?" He saw the way her leg curved and lengthened into thigh. "Terriss isn't the kind of guy you look up. He's the kind you run into." She had taken another cigarette into her mouth. He crossed to light it. Her perfume was of flesh as he bent over her, and her eyes were wide and bold. It was too soon. He snapped shut the lighter, but he stood over her for a moment longer, smelling her. "You won't change your mind about a drink?"

"It's food I want." She didn't want food. She wanted what he wanted.

"You'll get it," he told her. But not yet. He was comfortable. He didn't want to start out again. He wanted to sit here opposite her, feeling for knowledge of her in his mind. He knew her; he had known her on that first evening when he'd bumped into her. But it was satisfying to corroborate the knowledge. He said, "First, I'm going to have a drink."

She gave in. "Make it two."

He smiled to himself as he went to the kitchen. He'd thought she would change her mind. A couple of drinks and they'd get acquainted faster. When he returned to the living room with the drinks, she was still curved in the chair. As if she hadn't stirred but were waiting for him to infuse movement into her.

She had moved. The paper his foot had trodden was by her chair. She took the glass from him, and she said, "I see where the strangler's been at it again." She wasn't very interested; it was conversation, nothing more. "Someday maybe those dopes will learn not to pick up strange men."

"You picked me up."

She'd taken a long swallow of the highball. As he spoke, she lifted her eyebrows. "You picked me up, Princeton." She purred, "Besides, you're no stranger." She knew it too, the instinct of one for the other. "Mel's liquor is good as ever."

He said, "Yes, he left a good cellar for me." He went on, "I ran into him in a bar."

"And you had an old-home week."

"He was potted and trying to make my girl." His eyes spoke meaning beyond the words he slurred. "A blonde."

60

"That you'd picked up somewhere," she retorted.

He lied, "Friend of mine from home. She was just here for a week. Not Mel's type." He drank. He couldn't even remember the girl or her name. "Did you ever try to get rid of Mel when he was soused?"

"When wasn't he?"

"Well," he shrugged. "I promised to lunch with him next day. I lunched with him. I was trying to find an apartment. He was going to Rio on this new job. So—"

"Wait a minute," she called out. "Not Mel. Not a job in Rio."

"That's what he told me," Dix said. That's what Mel had said. He could have gone on a job. Some alcoholics tried to make a new start.

She was laughing to herself. "So you moved in."

"Yes, I moved in." He wasn't irritated. She didn't mean he was a charity case; she wouldn't be here drinking with him if she didn't think he had the stuff to spend. She probably thought he was another stinking rich loafer like Mel Terriss. He was casual. "I needed a quiet place for my work."

She was still laughing within her. "What do you do? Invent bombs?"

"I'm a writer." He didn't let her put the question. It was time again for her to answer questions. "I suppose you're in pictures?"

"Not often. I don't like getting up mornings." She knew all the tricks, to speak in commonplace phrases, to say more than words could say. He wondered who was keeping her. He could see the guy, fat-paunched, fat-jowled, balding. Too old, too ugly to get without paying for it. Paying plenty. A guy with nothing on his side but money. A bad idea slapped him. Could Terriss have been the guy? He didn't fit the picture of Old Moneybags. But if you revised the picture. A younger fellow, dopey with drink, his looks ravaged by the booze, a dullard always, even before alcohol narcotized what he had for a brain. And that stinking ego. He could just hear Terriss boasting about his girl, wearing her in public the way she wore that hunk of a ring; making himself believe he didn't have to buy it, he was just treating the gal right.

It couldn't have been Terriss. Terriss would have bragged about her. At least he'd have mentioned her. It wasn't Terriss. But doubts were worms crawling in his mind. She could twist a man about those taloned fingers, a man like Terriss. She could have excuses to keep her name out of it. Her career. A jealous ex. A divorce not quite complete.

She hadn't been talking. She'd been having her drink, eyeing him. Nor had his thoughts run across his face. It was trained to remain emotionless.

He finished his drink. "I don't like mornings either," he said. "That's why I'm a writer."

"Trying to break into pictures?"

He laughed at her. "I write books, lady. When I try to break into screen work, it will be because I need the money." He'd said the right thing, some of the speculation about him went out of her that quickly. There was an imperceptible relaxing of her muscular tension. He watched her over the edge of his glass as he tilted it, finished his drink. "Another?"

"Not now—"

He broke in, "I know, you're hungry. Wait'll I get a jacket and we'll be on our way." He didn't take a minute, catching up the heavy tweed jacket, a fuzzy, wiry tweed, rich brown, rich stuff. He slipped into the coat—he had about twenty dollars, enough for a Sunday-night dinner. Not a dress-up dinner, not in slacks.

She had retouched her lips, combed out her hair, resettled the white coat over the yellow sweater. She looked as fresh as if she'd just tubbed. She turned from the mirror as he reentered, the mirror near the desk. Her bag was on the desk. Good thing he'd mailed Uncle Fergus's letter. She was the kind who wouldn't care how she got her information on a man.

"Ready?"

She nodded, and she walked towards the door. He came up behind her. In time to open the door. She looked up at him. "Do you have Mel's address in Rio?" The question was sudden. Why the hell couldn't she forget Mel Terriss?

"I'll give it to you when we get back," he told her. He opened the door. They went together into the night.

He touched her then for the first time, his hand against her elbow, escorting her into the blue courtyard.

He asked, "How would you like to drive up to Malibu?"

# Chapter Three

## 1

SHE wasn't afraid. She rested herself carelessly against the seat of the car, her left knee half-turned towards his thigh. In the rounding of a corner she would touch him. She knew it; she curled herself deliberately in this fashion. It was one of her tricks. Yet, even knowing it was a trick, he was stimulated, waiting for that pressure.

This was the beginning of something good, so good that he was enjoying its immediacy without thought, without plan. She was beside him; that was enough. He had needed her for so long a time. He had always needed her.

It was a dream. A dream he had not dared dream, a woman like this. A tawny-haired woman; a high-breasted, smooth-hipped, scented woman; a wise woman. He didn't want to go to Malibu, he wanted to swing the car around, return to the apartment. He could wait. It was better to wait. She knew that.

The traffic lanes were quieter at this early evening hour. He followed Wilshire to the eucalyptus grove of San Vicente. The spice of eucalyptus scented the darkness. San Vicente was a dark street; he hadn't noticed before. And the smell of the sea came in to meet them long before they reached the hill that dropped into the canyon, long before they reached the sound of the sea.

She was quiet on the drive. He was grateful for her quietness. He wondered if she were feeling for knowledge of him in her quietness or if she were only tired. She didn't speak until he turned into the canyon.

She remarked then, "You know the back roads."

"You recognize them," he smiled.

The touch of her knee on his thigh was more deliberate. She tossed back her hair. "I've driven them often enough," she said in that slow, husky way which gave words meaning. She laughed. "I've friends in Malibu."

"The particular friend?"

"Which one?" she countered.

"Isn't there a particular one?" Curiosity nagged him. He wanted to know about her. But he couldn't ask questions, not open questions. She was like him; she'd lie.

"There usually is," she said. They had reached the ocean road, turn right to Malibu. "Where will we eat?"

"Any place you say. You know Malibu."

"I don't want to go to Malibu."

He turned his head, puzzled at her abruptness. Afraid for the moment that this was to be the end of it, that she would put him off as she had the other man. Afraid that he'd said the wrong thing or done the wrong thing, although he didn't know where he'd gone wrong. But she was still relaxed. She said, "I'm too hungry to drive that far. Let's stop at Carl's."

Anything that she said. The neon sign of Carl's slatted over the road ahead. He remembered the Nicolais and their friends had mentioned a Carl's or Joe's or Sam's. He wouldn't want to run into them. He wanted Laurel alone, unshared. Not touched by the anger and terror which entangled the Nicolais. He didn't ever want her touched by ugly things.

Yet he had no reason to reject Carl's. No reason to instill controversy in what had been between them, quiet, uncluttered. If Carl's had been the Nicolais' dinner choice, they would be gone by now. It had been more than two hours since he left them; they were planning to eat at that time. A car was pulling out from the front of the restaurant. Instinct avoided the lights. He drew up in the road at the side of the building, parked there.

She said, "I'll slide through." He stood there watching her come to him, taking her hand, touching her waist as he helped her from the car. The sea was a surge and a hush in the darkness across the road. She stood close to him for a moment, too close, before he removed his hand. She said, "You don't mind stopping here? The shrimp's good."

She led him around to the steps, and they went up into the dining room. There were few in it. His quick look saw that he knew no one. Nor did she. Her look was quick as his own.

It was a spacious room, warm with light, circled with windows overlooking the dark sea. They sat facing each other, and it was good. To be with a woman. To be opposite her, to have his fill of her face, the shape of it, the texture of it, the bone structure beneath the amber flesh. The set of her eyes and the shape of her mouth . . . her fire-tipped mouth.

"You think you'll know me the next time you see me?"

He returned to her actuality. He laughed, but his words weren't made of laughter. "I knew you before I ever saw you."

Her eyes widened.

"And you knew me."

She let her lashes fall. They curved long as a child's, russet against her cheeks. She said, "You're pretty sure of yourself, aren't you, Dix?"

"Never before."

Her eyes opened full again, and laughter echoed through her. "Oh, brother!" she breathed.

He didn't answer her, only with the look in his eyes. He hadn't been sure-footed with her before. He was now. He knew how to play it. She was brittle only on the surface. Underneath she too was seeking. Exhilaration heightened him. He knew then the rightness of this; she was for him.

The waitress came to the table before he could further it. He said, "You order, Laurel. I'll double it. Drink first?" He was irritated by the interruption. The waitress was a little chit, too much hair and flat face.

"No drinks." Laurel ordered for both, competently, without fuss. "Bring the coffee now, will you?"

The waitress went away, but she was back too quickly. She poured the coffee. This time she'd be away longer.

Laurel said, "If you don't want your coffee now, I'll drink both, Princeton."

"You're out of luck." She knew what a man wanted, coffee, now, not later. He lighted her cigarette, realizing her as he leaned across the table. She was real, not a begging dream in his loneness. She was a woman.

She settled herself in comfort. "How long have you been living at Mel's place?" She was deliberately veering from intimacy. It didn't matter; postponement added zest.

He tried to remember. "About two months—six weeks, I guess."

"Funny I haven't run into you."

"Yes." Yet it wasn't. He'd used the back door, shortcut to the garage. He hadn't been in the blue patio half a dozen times. "I thought you were a visitor when I bumped into you last night. Have you been away?"

"No."

"Guess our hours didn't coincide. They will now."

"They might," she admitted.

"They will," he said with certainty.

Again she veered. "When did Mel leave?"

He figured it in his mind. "August. Around about the first. Before I moved in."

The waitress divided them again. She wasn't too long about it, and she was agreeable despite her flat face. The shrimp looked good, and she poured more coffee without request.

He waited only until she was out of hearing. "Why the interest in Mel? I thought you'd only been in his place a couple of times." It wasn't jealousy, but she'd think there was a twinge of it in him. She was thinking it now, maybe that was why she kept harping on Mel. Just another trick, not actual curiosity. "You weren't carrying the torch there?"

"Good Lord, Princeton!" That ended that. She needn't try that trick again.

He smiled slightly. "I was beginning to think he might have been the jeweler." His forefinger touched the mass of gold and ruby.

Her lip curled. "Mel was more careful of his money than that. Liquor was the only thing he could bear to spend it on." Her eyes touched the ring. "My ex."

He lifted his eyebrows. "It's a nice piece."

She said suddenly, "Don't ever marry money. It isn't worth it." She began to eat as if her hunger had reawakened.

"I've always thought it might be a good racket." He added, "For a woman."

"There's nothing wrong with the money. It's what goes with it." Her face was stony. "Bastards."

"Exes?"

"Rich men. And women. They believe the earth was created for them. They don't have to think or feel—all they have to do is buy it. God, how I hate them!" She shook her head. "Shut up, Laurel."

He smiled patiently. "I don't believe that's true of all of them."
As if he were a rich guy himself, one of the dirty bastards himself.

She said, "I can smell them a mile off. They're all alike."

"They aren't all like Mel—or your ex."

She went on eating. As if she hadn't heard him. And he had to
know. If Mel had been in on the rent. He seized it. "After all they
pay the rent. And the jeweler."

"They don't pay mine," she said savagely. Then she smiled. "I
said shut up, Laurel. But I'm surprised Mel went off without saying good-bye. He was always in my hair."

"I'm surprised he didn't take you with him," Dix said.

She grimaced. "I told you I'd learned my lesson. Don't marry
money."

No one was paying her rent. She was on her own; the ex, the
rich one, must have settled up. She'd see to that; she and a battery
of expensive lawyers. He said lightly, "It's the man who pays and
pays. It couldn't have been too bad. You can sleep mornings and
not have to worry about the roof over your head."

She said, "Yes," and the hardness came about her mouth. "As
long as I don't marry again."

He understood her bitterness, but, understanding, he was disturbed. There could be someone she wanted, the way he was going to want her. She wouldn't have the hatred of the ex if there
weren't a reason; she had his money to live on and free of him.
Dix couldn't go on asking questions; he'd asked too many now.
He was prying, and she'd know it when the anger went out of her.
He smiled at her again. "I'm glad that's the way it is," he said.

"Why?" She flashed at him.

"Because I wouldn't have found you in time—if it hadn't been
that way."

Because she was desired, she softened. Giving him the look and
the dare. She said, "Why, Princeton!"

"Or am I in time?"

She smiled, the inscrutable smile of a woman who knew the ways of a woman. She didn't answer him. There could be someone else. But at the moment, here with her, he was sure of his own prowess. Because he knew this was intended; that he and she should meet and in meeting become enmeshed. It was to be; it was.

They were the last guests to leave the restaurant. Again in the dark, sea-scented night, he was filled with power and excitement and rhythm. But tonight it was good. Because he was with her.

He didn't want to turn back to the city. He wanted to go on with her into this darkness, with the sound of water echoing the beat of his heart. He wanted to keep her with him always in this oneness of the two. He wanted to lift her with him into the vastness of the night sky. He said, "Shall we drive on up to Malibu?"

But he didn't want to drive; he didn't want to be occupied with the mechanics of a car. He was relieved when she refused.

"Let's keep away from Malibu."

He turned back, but driving without plan, he found the place where he could silence the car. An open stretch overlooking the dark beach and the sea. He said, "Do you mind? I just want to smell the salt."

Her eyebrows quirked. She'd thought he was parking the way a kid parked with his girl. She liked it that he hadn't meant it for that. She said suddenly, "Let's go down where we can really smell it."

The wind caught at them as they left the car and descended to the beach. The wind and the deep sand pushed at them, but they struggled on, down to the water's edge. Waves were frost on the dark churning waters. Stars pricked through the curved sky. The rhythm pulsed; the crash and the slurring swish repeated endlessly; the smell of the sea was sharp. Spindrift salted their lips.

He had taken her hand as they walked to the water. He held it now, and she didn't withdraw it from his. She said, "I haven't done this for a long, long time." Her voice wasn't brittle; she wasn't playing a game with him. She was alone here, with him but alone. The wind swirled her hair across her face until he could see only the slant of her forehead and her cheek. Happiness rose like a spire within him. He hadn't expected ever to know happiness again. His voice stirred, "Laurel—"

She turned her head, slowly, as if surprised that he was there. The wind blew her hair like mist across her face. She lifted her face, and for the first time, there in the light of the sea and the stars, he knew the color of her eyes. The color of dusk and mist rising from the sea, with the amber of stars flecking them.

"Laurel," he said, and she came to him the way he had known from the beginning it must be. "Laurel," he cried, as if the word were the act. And there became a silence around them, a silence more vast than the thunderous ecstasy of the hungry sea.

# 2

*To SLEEP, perchance to dream and dreaming wake* . . . To sleep and to wake. To sleep in peace, without the red evil of dreaming. To wake without need to struggle through fog to reach the sunlight. To find sleep good and waking more good. It was the ringing phone that woke him. He reached for it, and he felt her stir beside him.

He spoke into it quietly, not wishing to wake her. Yet he willed her to wake, to open her eyes as he had opened his, into the full sunshine. "Hello."

"Dix? Did I interrupt your work?"

It was Brub Nicolai. For the instant there was a waning of the sun, as if a cold hand had pushed against it. Dix softened his voice to answer. "Not at all."

Brub didn't sound depressed today; it could have been the old

Brub speaking. "Who was that redhead I seen you with last night? Was that the redhead?"

He couldn't answer quickly. It was impossible for Brub to have seen him last night with Laurel. Unless Brub were having him followed. That was more impossible. That would be incredible. He asked, "What are you talking about?"

"The redhead, Dickson. Not the blonde you were meeting in Hollywood. The redhead. Was that—"

Dix said, "Hm, a Peeping Tom. Where were you hiding, Tom?"

Brub laughed. As if he hadn't a care in the world. "You didn't see us. We were pulling out of Carl's when you went in. It was Sylvia spotted you. I spotted the redhead."

The car he had avoided by parking at the side of the building. There were always eyes. A little tailor on his way home from a movie. A waitress in a drive-in. A butcher boy on a bicycle. A room clerk with a wet pointed nose. A detective's wife who was alert, too alert. Whose eyes saw too much.

There were always eyes, but they didn't see. He had proved it. His hand relaxed on the phone. "You would. And what did the little woman say to that?"

"I couldn't repeat such language." There was an imperceptible change in Brub's voice. Back to business. "How about lunch with me? You bring the redhead."

He could hear the stir of her breath. She was awake, but she was silent. "She's tied up." He wouldn't put her and Brub together. She belonged in a different compartment from the Nicolais.

"Then you're not, I take it. How about lunch?"

He could refuse. But he didn't want to. Even to be with her. Because the game with Brub was important; it had to be played. There was renewed zest of the game in having Brub make the approach today.

"Sure," he agreed. "What time and where?" He noted the clock. It was past eleven.

"Noon? I'm at the Beverly Hills station."

His pulse leaped. The game was growing better. To walk into the police station, to be the guest of Homicide for lunch. But he didn't want to hurry. He wanted to watch her rise from sleep, to see her woman-ways, the clothing of her, the combing of her hair. He asked, "Can you make it one or do you punch a time clock?"

"One's okay. Meet me here?"

"I'll be there, Brub." He replaced the phone and turned to look on her. She was beautiful. She was younger than he'd thought her on first meeting; she was beautiful in the morning after sleep. Her hair was cobweb on the pillow; her dusky amber-flecked eyes were wide. She didn't smile up at him; she looked at him with that long, wondering look.

She said, "Who's first on the shower?"

He put his fingers to her cheek. He wanted to tell her how beautiful she was. He wanted to tell her all that she was to him, all that she must be. He said, "The one who doesn't fix the coffee."

She stirred, lazy as a cat. "I don't cook."

"Then you do the scrubbing, lady. And don't take all day."

"You have a lunch date," she mocked.

"Business."

"It sounded like it."

He didn't dare touch her, not if he were to make it to Brub. He slid away his fingers, slowly, with reluctance. Yet there was a pleasure in the reluctance, in the renunciation. This moment would come again, and he would not let it pass. Postponing it would make it the sweeter.

"Go on," she urged. "Make the coffee."

She didn't believe that he meant to leave. He surprised her when he rose obediently, wrapped his bathrobe about him. He wanted to surprise her; he wanted her interest. She knew men so well, although she was too young to know so well. Only by whetting her interest would she remain with him long enough to become entangled with him. Because she was spoiled and wise and suspicious.

He put on the coffee in the kitchen, and then he went to the front door. The paper had hit the doorstep today; he didn't have to step outside for it. It was habit that unfolded it and looked at the front page. He didn't really care what was on it. The story wasn't there; it was on the second page, the police quizzing friends of the dead Mildred, the police admitting this early that there were no leads. He read the story scantly. He could hear the downpour of the shower. There was no mail in the slot. Too soon to hear from Uncle Fergus. The old buzzard had better come through. He'd need money to take Laurel where she should be taken. To expensive places where she could be displayed as she should be.

He flung down the paper, went back to the bedroom, impatient to see her again. She was still in the bathroom, but the shower was turned off. He called, "How do you take your coffee?" Touching the soft yellow of her sweater there on the chair. Wanting to look on her, to smell her freshness.

She opened the door. She was wrapped in a borrowed white terry bathrobe. It was a cocoon enfolding her. Her face was shining, and her damp hair was massed on top of her head. She came to the quick take of his breath, came to him and he held her. "Oh, God," he said. Deliberately he set her away. "I've got a business luncheon in one hour. How do you want your coffee?"

Her eyes slanted. "Sweet and black."

He hurried as she sat down at the dressing table, hurried to return to her. She was still there when he brought the coffee. She was combing out her hair, her fiery gold hair. He put the coffee down for her, and he carried his own across the room.

"You'd better shower, Dix. You don't want to be late for that business appointment."

"It is business. Someday I'll tell you all about it." He drank his

75

coffee, watching the way she swirled her hair below her shoulders. Watching the way she painted her lips, brushed her lashes. As if she belonged here. Jealousy flecked him. She knew her way around, had she been here before? He couldn't bear it if Mel Terriss had touched her. Yet he knew she had been touched by other men; there was no innocence in her.

Abruptly he left her, long enough to shower. He couldn't stay with her, not with the anger rising in him. It washed away in the shower. Mel Terriss wasn't here. She couldn't have had anything to do with Terriss. She wouldn't ever have been that hard up. He opened the door when he'd finished showering, fearing that she might have slipped away from him. But she was there, almost in the doorway. "I brought you more coffee," she said.

"Thanks, baby. Mind the noise of a razor?"

"I can take it." She was dressed now. She sat on the edge of the tub with her coffee, watching him shave. As if she couldn't bear to leave him. As if it was the same with her as with him. The burring didn't annoy him with her there. He could talk through it, gaily. "I knew you'd be busy. That's why I said okay."

"And if I weren't?"

"Aren't you?"

"I have a voice lesson at two," she admitted.

"What time will you be home?"

"Why?" she mocked.

He didn't bother to answer, only with his eyes. He finished shaving, cleaned the razor. "Busy tonight?"

"Why?" she repeated.

"I might be free," he said.

"Call me."

"I'll camp on your doorstep."

She frowned slightly, ever so slightly. He might have imagined it. Only she said, "I'll come here." And she curved her lips. "If I'm free."

76

She didn't want him to come to her place. It could be the ex, yet how could it be? It could be she was tied up with someone else. She could have lied. There might be a Mr. Big in the background. The man she'd lied to last night.

He said definitely, "If you aren't here, I'll be on your doorstep."

She followed him into the bedroom again, lounged on the edge of the bed while he dressed. Gray slacks, a blue shirt—he wouldn't need a coat; warmth filled the room. From the back of the chair he took the tweed jacket he'd worn last night. He'd forgotten to hang it.

She said, "That looks like Mel's jacket. He was a good dresser."

He turned with it in his hands. She hadn't meant anything. It was just a remark. He admitted, "It's Mel's," casually but boldly. "In Rio it's summer. Mel was going to buy up all the best Palm Beach. He left his old stuff here, told me to help myself." He explained it, continuing into the closet, the closet filled with Mel's expensive clothes. "My own things shrank when I was in the service. And thanks to the shortages, I arrived here practically destitute."

She said, "I'm surprised anything of Mel's would fit you."

He closed the closet door. "His backlog before he developed that paunch. He was skinny enough at Nassau."

He transferred his billfold and car keys.

She said, "He even left you his car. You must have done him a favor once. I never thought he'd give away an old toothpick."

He smiled. "He's making up for all of it on the sublease. But I did do him several favors."

"At Nassau," she mimicked.

"Yeah. I used to speak to him." He took her arm, steered her to the door. "Is your phone still disconnected?"

"Why?"

"Because I'll start calling you the minute I'm back here."

"I'll call you when I get back."

They were at the front door, and she turned to him, into his arms. Her mouth was like her hair, flame. This time she broke from him. "You have a business date," she reminded.

"Yeah." He took his handkerchief, wiped his lips. "Somebody might be in that empty patio."

She laughed. "The nice part about departing at noon, Dix, is that no one knows what time you arrived."

They left together, and he heard her footsteps passing the pool to her staircase. He knew he was behaving like a love-smitten sophomore, but he waited by the entrance until she was on her balcony, until she lifted her hand to him in good-bye.

He'd left his car standing in the street. There hadn't been time last night to put it away. He was pleased it was there, that he didn't have to go through the back alley to get it out. He felt too good to do more than step into it and swing away on its power. He was even on time for the appointment with Brub.

He drove up Beverly Drive, turning over to the city hall. It looked more like a university hall than headquarters for the police, a white-winged building with a center tower. It was set in green grass, bordered with shrubs and flowers. There was nothing about it that said police save that the huge bronze lamps on either side of the door burned green. He climbed the stone steps and entered the door.

The corridor inside was clean and businesslike. A sign directed to the police quarters. He went up to the desk. It might have been the desk in any office. If it hadn't been for the dark blue uniform of the man just leaving, it would be hard to believe this was the Beverly Hills police station. The pleasant young man behind the desk wore a brown plaid sports coat and tan slacks.

Dix said, "Brub Nicolai?" He didn't know a title. "Detective Nicolai. He's expecting me."

He followed the young man's directions up the hall, entered another businesslike room. Brub was sitting in a chair. There were a couple of other men present, a little older than Brub, in plain business suits. They didn't look any different than ordinary men. They were L.A. Homicide.

Brub's face brightened when he saw Dix. "You made it."

"I'm seven minutes early."

"And I'm hungry." Brub turned to the other men, the tall, lean one and the smaller, heavier-set one. "See you later." He didn't introduce Dix. But they were Homicide. It was in the way their eyes looked at a man, even a friend of one of their own. Memorizing him. Brub said, "Come on, Dix. Before I start eating the leg of a chair."

Dix said, "Sawdust will give you a bay window if you aren't careful."

They walked down the corridor, out into the sunshine. "My car's here."

Brub said, "Might as well walk. We can't park much nearer. Where do you usually eat?"

"If you're hungry and don't want to stand in line, we'll go to my favorite delicatessen. Or the Ice House."

They walked together the few blocks. The sun was warm, and the air smelled good. It was like a small town, the unhurried workers of the village greeting each other in the noon, standing on the corners talking in the good-smelling sunshine. He chose the Ice House; it was the nearer, just around the corner on Beverly. Man-food in it. He was surprised that he too had an appetite. Good sleep meant good appetite.

He grinned across the table at Brub. "For a moment this morning you startled me. I thought you were clairvoyant."

"About your redhead?" Brub whistled. "That's a piece of goods. How did you arrange to meet her?"

He could talk of her to Brub. And like a love-smitten swain he wanted to talk of her. "It's time the Virginibus Arms had a good-neighbor policy."

"Virginibus Arms? Not bad," Brub said.

He realized then that Brub hadn't known his address until now. He'd given his phone number, not his address.

"Yeah, I was lucky. Sublease. From Mel Terriss." Brub didn't know Mel. "Fellow I went to school with at Princeton. Ran into him out here just when he was leaving on a job."

"Damn lucky," Brub said. "And the redhead went with it?"

He grinned again, like a silly ass. "Wish I'd known it sooner."

"Is she in pictures?"

"She's done a little." He knew so little about her. "She's studying."

"What's her name?"

Brub wasn't prying; this was the old Brub. Brub and Dix. The two Musketeers. A part of each other's lives.

"Laurel," he said, and saying the name, his heart quickened. "Laurel Gray."

"Bring her out some night. Sylvia would like to meet her."

"Sylvia, my eye. You don't think I'd expose Laurel to your wolfish charms, do you?"

"I'm married, son. I'm safe."

"Maybe. What about that little gal yesterday? Wasn't she cooing at you?"

Brub said, "Maude would coo at a pair of stilts. Cary's sort of a sixth cousin of Sylvia. That's why we get together. Maude thought you were wonderful, hero."

"Did she ever stop talking?"

"No, she never stops. Although after she saw you with Redhead, she subdued a bit."

It was good to know that it didn't matter how many saw him with Laurel. That he could appear with her everywhere, show her everywhere; there was no danger in it. Only he wouldn't take her to Nicolai's. Not to face Sylvia's cool appraisal. Sylvia would look at her through Sylvia's own standards, through long-handled eyeglasses.

"She was certainly hipped on your case," Dix said. It was time to steer the conversation. "How's it coming?"

"Dead end."

"You mean you're closing the books?"

"We don't ever close the books, Dix." Brub's face was serious. "After the newspapers and the Maudes and all the rest of them forget it, our books are open. That's the way it is."

"That's the way it has to be," Dix agreed as seriously.

"There've been tough cases before now. Maybe ten, twelve years the department has had to work on them. In the end we find the answer."

"Not always," Dix said.

"Not always," Brub admitted. "But more often than you'd think. Sometimes the cases are still unsolved on paper, but we have the answer. Sometimes it's waiting for the next move."

"The criminal doesn't escape." Dix smiled wryly.

Brub said, "I won't say that. Although I honestly don't think he ever does escape. He has to live with himself. He's caught there in that lonely place. And when he sees he can't get away—" Brub shrugged. "Maybe suicide, or the nuthouse—I don't know. But I don't think there's any escape."

"What about Jack the Ripper?"

"What about him? A body fished out of the river, an accident case. A new inmate of an asylum. Nobody knows. One thing you can know, he didn't suddenly stop his career. He was stopped."

Dix argued, "Maybe he did stop it. Maybe he'd had enough."

"He couldn't stop," Brub denied. "He was a murderer."

Dix lifted his eyebrows. "You mean a murderer is a murderer? As a detective is a detective? A waiter a waiter?"

"No. Those are selected professions. A detective or a waiter can change to another field. I mean a murderer is a murderer as . . . an actor is an actor. He can stop acting professionally, but he's still an actor. He acts. Or an artist. If he never picks up another brush, he will still see and think and react as an artist."

"I believe," Dix said slowly, "you could get some arguments on that."

"Plenty," Brub agreed cheerfully. "But that's the way I see it." He attacked his pie.

Dix put sugar in his coffee. Black and sweet. And hot. He smiled, thinking of her. "What about this new Ripper? You think he's a nut?"

"Sure," Brub agreed.

The quick agreement rankled. Brub should be brighter than that. "He's been pretty smart for a nut, hasn't he? No clues."

"That doesn't mean anything," Brub said. "The insane are much more clever about their business, and more careful too, than the sane. It's normal for them to be sly and secretive. That's part of the mania. It makes them difficult to catch up with. But they give themselves away."

"They do? How?"

"When is more important. But plenty of ways. Repetition of the pattern." Brub finished off the pie and lit a cigarette. "The pattern is clear enough with the strangler. It's the motive that's hard to fix on."

"Does an insane man need a motive? Does he have one?" He lit a cigarette.

"Within the mania, yes."

Dix said offside, "This is fascinating to me, Brub. You say you have the pattern. Doesn't that in a way incorporate the motive?"

"In a way, yes. But you take this case. The pattern has emerged. Not too clearly, but in a fuzzy way, yes. It's a girl alone. At night. She doesn't know the man. At least we're reasonably sure of that. This last girl, as far as we can find out, couldn't possibly have known the man. And there's no slight connection between the girls. All right then: it's a pickup. A girl waiting for a bus or walking home. He comes along in a car, and she accepts a ride."

"I thought you were figuring he didn't have a car. What were you talking about?"—he appeared to try to remember—"Going into a drive-in to eat—"

Brub broke in. "He had to have a car. Not in every case but definitely in the last ones." His eyes looked seriously into Dix's. "My own theory is that he doesn't make the approach from the car. Because girls are wary about getting into a car with strangers. The danger of that has been too well publicized. I think he makes the approach on foot, and after he has the lamb lulled, he mentions he's on his way to get his car. Take this last one. She's waiting for a bus. He's waiting on the same corner. Busses don't run often that time of night. They get talking. He invites her to have a cup of coffee. It was a foggy night, pretty chilly. By the time they've had coffee, he mentions his car isn't far away and he'll give her a lift."

Dix set down his coffee cup carefully. "That's how you're figuring it," he nodded his head. "It sounds reasonable." He looked at Brub again. "Do your colleagues agree?"

"They think I may be on the right track."

"And the motive?"

"That's anybody's guess." Brub scowled. "Maybe he doesn't like women. Maybe some girl did him dirt and he's getting even with all of them."

Dix said, "That sounds absurd." He laughed, "It wouldn't hold water in my book."

"You're forgetting. It's mania; not sanity. Now you or I, if we wanted to strike back at a girl, we'd get us another one. Show the other gal what she'd lost. But a mind off the trolley doesn't figure that way."

"Any other motives?" Dix laughed.

"Religious mania, perhaps. There've always been plenty of that kind of nut out here. But it all comes back to one focal point: the man is a killer; he has to kill. As an actor has to act."

"And he can't stop?" Dix murmured.

"He can't stop," Brub said flatly. He glanced at his watch. "I've got to go up Beverly Glen. Want to come along?"

Dix's eyebrows questioned.

"To the scene of the crime," Brub explained. "Would you like to have a look at it? It'll tell you more than I can in words of what we're working against."

His pulse leaped at the idea of it. To the scene of the crime. For book material. He said, "Yeah, I think I will." He glanced at his own watch. Two-twenty. "I can take another hour from work. Particularly since I can charge it up to research."

Brub picked up the checks. At Dix's demurring, he said, "This is on me. In the line of business."

The cold touch at the base of his spine was imaginary. He laughed. "You mean detectives have a swindle sheet? Authors aren't so lucky."

"I'll put it down: conferring with an expert." He queried, "All mystery authors claim to be crime experts, don't they?"

"I'll dedicate the book to the dick who bought me a lunch."

He and Brub emerged into the sunshine of Beverly Drive. The lunch hour was done; the workers had returned to their offices. Women shoppers were beginning to stroll the street. They clustered at the shopwindows. They held little children by the hand. They chattered as they went about their aimless female business. There wasn't a brilliant redhead in sight.

The news vendor on the corner talked the races with a passing customer. His folded papers, the early edition of the *News*, lay stacked on the sidewalk beside a cigar box holding coins. Dix's eyes fell to the papers, but he didn't buy one. There wouldn't be any fresh news anyway. He was with the source of news.

They returned to the city hall. "Shall we take your car or mine?" Brub asked.

The cold hand touched him quickly again. How could he know?

84

Brub couldn't be suspicious of him. There wasn't a shred of reason for thinking it. Brub included Dix with himself, "normal as you and I." Yet how could he be sure? Brub had once known him so well. That was long ago. No one could read him now. Not even Laurel.

Did Brub want him to take his car back up the Beverly Glen Canyon? Was this luncheon arranged? Were the two ordinary men, who were L.A. Homicide, waiting for Brub to report back to them? He had hesitated long enough in answering, too long. It couldn't matter which car. There couldn't be eyes waiting to identify a black coupe, a coupe like a thousand others. It couldn't be tire marks they were after; they were unable to get marks off a clean, paved road. Brub had said so. Had intimated so. Too many cars had passed that way.

He pretended to come to. "Did you say something? Sorry."

Brub grinned. "Thinking about the redhead? I said, whose car shall we take? Yours or mine?"

"It doesn't matter," he answered promptly. But he knew as he answered that he preferred to take his own. He'd been a pantywaist to have considered anything but that. That was what quickened his mind, that was what put zest into the game. To take the dare. "Might as well use mine."

Brub said, "Okay," but he stopped at the doors to the building. "I'll go in and see if Lochner wants to ride up with us. You don't mind another passenger?"

"Not at all." He followed Brub. To watch faces, to see if there were interchange of expression.

Only one of the Homicide men was left. He was talking to a couple of motorcycle cops in uniform. Talking about the local baseball club. Brub said, "Want to go up Beverly Glen, Loch?" He made the introductions then. "Jack Lochner—my friend, Dix Steele."

Lochner was the tall, thin man. His clothes were a little too big for him, as if he'd lost weight worrying. His face was lined. He looked like just an ordinary man, not too successful. He didn't give Brub any special glance. He didn't examine Dix now as he had earlier; he shook hands and said, "Nice to know you, Mr. Steele." His voice was tired.

Brub said, "Dix is a mystery writer, Loch. He wants to go along. You don't mind?"

"Not at all." Lochner tried to smile, but he wasn't a man used to smiling. Just used to worry. "Nothing to see. I don't know why we're going back. Except Brub wants to. And the Beverly Hills bunch seems to think he's on the right track."

Dix raised one eyebrow. "So you do have some ideas?"

Brub's laugh was embarrassed. "Don't you start riding me too. All I've got is a feeling."

"Psychic," Lochner droned.

"No," Brub denied fast. "But I can't help feeling we're on the right track here in Beverly." He explained to Dix, "The Beverly bunch sort of feels the same way. That's why we're hanging around here. Beverly has its own force, you know, separate from L.A., but they're doing everything they can to help us."

"And they know how to help," Loch said. "A smart bunch."

They left the building together. Dix said, "We're taking my car." He steered them to it. He wasn't going in a police car. Only a man off his trolley would consider riding around in a police car with Homicide. Homicide with psychic hunches.

"Do you know the way?" Lochner asked.

"I know where Beverly Glen is. You can direct me from there." With the dare taken, his mind was sharp, cold and clear and sharp as a winter wind back East. They could direct. Not a muscle would twitch to indicate he knew the place. He began laughing to himself. Actually he didn't know the place. He didn't even have to worry about making the unwary move.

"Go over to Sunset," Brub directed. "Turn right on Beverly Glen."

"That much I know." He swung the car easily towards Sunset, enjoying the power of the motor, the smoothness of the drive. A good car. He held it back. You shouldn't speed up with cops in your car. "There were a couple of cops guarding the portals when I went by Sunday. On my way home after I left your place, Brub." Were those the same cops Lochner had had in the office? Were they there to look him over? He was getting slap-happy. The cops couldn't have picked him out of all the drivers passing that intersection Sunday afternoon. Just him, one man. His fingers tightened on the wheel. Did the police know more than they had told? Had there been someone else in the canyon on Friday night? He went on talking, "What were they doing? Waiting for the killer to return to the scene of the crime?"

"They were checking traffic," Lochner said in his disinterested voice. "I never knew a killer yet who went back. Make it easy for us if they did. We wouldn't have to beat our brains out all over town."

"All we'd have to do was post a couple of the boys and wait," Brub enlarged. "They could play checkers until he came along— easy."

"How would you know him from the sightseers?" Dix joined the game.

"That is an angle." Brub looked at Lochner.

The older man said, "He'd be the one who was too normal."

"No fangs? No drooling?" Dix laughed.

"Of course, he wouldn't know the cops were watching," Brub said.

They'd reached Beverly Glen, and Dix turned right. "You can direct me now."

"Just keep on going," Brub said. "We'll tell you when."

It was a pretty little road to start, rather like a New England lane with the leaves turning and beginning to fall from the trees. He had no tension, perhaps a slight fear that he might recognize the place, that muscular reaction might be transferred from him to Brub seated close beside him. He relaxed. He said, "This reminds me of home. Autumn in New York, or Connecticut, or Massachusetts."

"I'm from the East myself," Lochner said. "I've been away twenty years."

It wasn't pretty for long. A few estates and it became a road of shacks, little places such as men built in the mountains before the rich discovered their privacy and ousted them. And then the shacks were left behind and the road became a curving pass through the canyon to some valley beyond.

It would be lonely up here at night; there were deep culverts, heavy brush on the side of the road. It was lonely up here now, and they passed no cars. It was as if they had entered into a forbidden valley, a valley guarded by the police. Keeping the sightseers away. Only the hunters and the hunted allowed to enter. The walls of the canyon laid shadows over the road. There was a chill in the air; the sun was far away.

He drove on, waiting for them to give the word to stop. They weren't talking, either of them; they were on the case now, a case that had them angry and bitter and worried. He kept quiet; it wasn't the time for a conversation piece. He realized his fingers were tightened on the wheel, and again he relaxed them. He didn't know if the detectives would shout a sudden stop command or if they'd give warning or just how it would be done. He kept the speed down to twenty, and he watched the road ahead, not the culverts with leaves like brown droppings in them. He didn't recognize any of the road. That was the good part of it.

It was Lochner who said, "Here we are. Just pull up along here, Mr. Steele, if you will."

This stretch of the road was no different from the others. There was nothing marking it as the place where a girl had been found.

The detectives got out, and he got out on the other side of the car. He walked beside them across the road. "He came this far, and then he turned around," Brub said. "Or he may have been on his way back to town."

"This is where you found her?" Dix wasn't nervous. He was an author in search of material, a man along just for the ride.

Brub had stepped up into the rustling brown leaves. He said, "It's a little heavier here. He could have known that. He could have figured she wouldn't be found for a long time, with the leaves falling on her, covering her."

Brub was scuffing through the rustle, as if he expected to find something under the sound. A clue. An inspiration. "Every day there'd be more leaves. Not many people look off at the side of the road when they're driving. Not unless there's something scenic there. Nothing scenic about this thicket."

Lochner stood with his hands in his pockets, with the worry lines in his tired face. Stood beside Dix.

Dix could ask questions. He was supposed to ask questions. He said, "How was it she was found so quickly then?"

"Luck," Brub said. He stood in the ditch, leaves to his ankles. "The milkman had a flat right at this point."

Lochner said, "He picked this place on purpose."

"The milkman?" Dix looked incredulous.

"The killer. Take a look at it. The way the road curves here—he can see any lights coming from behind, two loops below. And he can look up to the top of the hill, see the lights of a car approaching him when it makes the first of those two curves. He can sit with her in the car, looking like a spooner, until the other car goes by." His eyes squinted up the road and back down again. "Not much chance of traffic here in the middle of the night. He was pretty safe." His voice had no inflection. "He does it. He opens the door of the car and rolls her out, and he's away. No chance of being caught at it. Strangling's the easiest way. And the safest."

Brub had stooped and brushed aside the leaves.

Dix moved closer to the edge of the thicket, looked up at him. "Find something?" he asked with the proper cheerful curiosity.

Lochner monotoned, "The experts have been over every inch with a microscope. He won't find anything. Only he wanted to come back up, so I said I'd come along." He put a cigarette in his mouth, cupped his hands about the match. "The only place we'll find anything is in his car."

A wind had come up, a small sharp wind. Lochner wouldn't have cupped the match if it hadn't. It wasn't imaginary. Dix said, with the proper regret, "And you've not been able to get a description of the car yet?"

"Not yet," Lochner said. In that tired way, but there was a tang underneath the inflection. Not yet, but they would. Because they never closed the books. Because a murderer had to murder. Dix wanted to laugh. They knew so little, with all their science and intuition; they were babes in toyland.

"When you do, you mean you might find a hairpin or a lipstick or something?"

Brub did laugh. There in the brush it sounded hollow. "Good Lord, Dix. You're old hat. Girls don't wear hairpins. You ought to know that."

"Dust," Lochner said.

"Dust?" He was puzzled now.

Brub climbed down from the thicket, one big step down. He began brushing the crumpled brown leaves from his trouser legs.

"That's dust," Lochner said. He turned back to the car. "We've got dust from the drive-in. We've got the dust from her clothes and her shoes. There'll be some of that same dust in his car."

Dix held the mask over his face. He shook his head, his expression one of awe and admiration. "And even if it's ten or twelve years, the dust will be the same?"

"Some of it will," Lochner said.

They all got back in the car. Dix started the engine. He asked, "Is there a better place to turn than here?" They were supposed to know. The police cars had been all over this territory. They'd drawn circles around it and carried laboratory technicians into it. They'd done everything but dig it up and carry it to headquarters.

"Go on a bit," Brub said. "There's a side road a little further on."

Dix ran the car up the hill. He saw the side road, and he turned in. The side road wasn't paved. If there were any suspicion, this could be a trap to check on his tires. Behind the brush, there could be the two cops, playing checkers, watching. Cops with plaster, ready to make casts. But they were wrong. He hadn't turned here before. There was a better place further on. He maneuvered the car. Headed back towards town.

He could be talkative now. He was supposed to be impressed and curious. He said, "Did you find anything, Brub?"

Brub shook his head. "No. I didn't expect to. It's just—I get closer to him when I do what he did. What he might have done. I've got a picture of him, but it's—it's clouded over. It's like seeing a man in the fog. The kind of a fog that hangs in our canyon."

Dix said cheerfully, "The kind you had when I was out at your place Friday night."

"Yeah," Brub said.

Lochner said, "He's from the East."

Dix's nerves were in strict control. Not one nerve end twitched. Rather he was stimulated by the sharp and cold blade of danger. He said, "That's a bit of information you've kept to yourselves, isn't it? Did the waitress recognize an Eastern accent?"

"It isn't information," Brub answered. "He talked just like any-body else. No accent. No particular quality of voice. That's Loch's reconstruction."

Lochner repeated, "He's from the East. I know that." He was deliberate. "He's a mugger."

"What's a mugger?" Dix asked quickly.

"Certain gangs used to operate in New York," Brub explained. He illustrated on himself with his right arm. "One man would get the victim so, the others would rob him. Until they found out it could be a one-man job. You don't need more than two fingers to strangle a man. Or woman."

"He's a mugger," Lochner repeated. "He doesn't use his fingers. There's no finger marks. He uses his arm. He's from the East."

Dix said, "As a fellow Easterner, Mr. Lochner, you might admit that a Westerner could have learned the trick."

Lochner repeated, "I've seen the way they did it in New York. He knows how. The same way."

They came out of the shadowed canyon, out into the sunshine, into the city again. But the sun had faded. There were clouds graying the blueness of sky. And the winding road of Sunset to Beverly was heavy with shadows of the late afternoon. It was almost four o'clock when they reached the city hall.

Dix pulled up and Lochner got out. He intoned, "Thanks for the lift, Mr. Steele."

Dix said, "Thank you for letting me go along." He shook his head. "It's pretty gruesome though. I don't think I'd go for police work."

Lochner walked away to the hall. Brub leaned against the car door. He was frowning. "It isn't pleasant," he said. "It's damned unpleasant. But it's there. You can't just close your eyes and pretend it isn't. There are killers, and they've got to be caught, they've got to be stopped. I don't like killing. I saw too much of it, same as you did. I hated it then, the callous way we'd sit around and map out our plans to kill people. People who didn't want to die any more than we wanted to die. And we'd come back afterwards and talk it over, check over how many we'd got that night. As if we'd been killing ants, not men." His eyes were intense. "I hate killers. I want the world to be a good place, a safe place. For me and my wife and my friends, and my kids when I have them. I guess that's why I'm a policeman. To help make one little corner of the world a safer place."

Dix said, "That's like you, Brub." He meant it. It didn't matter how unpleasant a job was, Brub would take it on if in the end it meant the righting of something wrong.

Brub pushed back his hat. He laughed, a short laugh. "Junior G-man rides his white horse. I suppose in a couple of years I'll be as stale as Loch. But right now it's personal. I want to get that killer." His laugh repeated. It was apology for his emotion. He said, "Hang around till I check in, and I'll buy you a drink."

"Sorry." Dix put his hands on the wheel. "I'm late now. We'll do it again. And thanks for a valuable afternoon, Brub."

"Okay, fellow. See you soon." Brub's hand lifted, and he rolled off, like a sailor on the sea. Like a policeman tracking an unknown foe.

# Chapter Four

## 1

HE RANG Laurel as soon as he reached the apartment. Before he fixed a drink, before even lighting a cigarette. There was no answer to the call. He rang her every fifteen minutes after that, and at six, when the dusk was moving across the open windows, and when there was still no answer to his call, he stepped out into the courtyard where he could look up at her apartment. But there were no lights in it.

His toe stubbed the evening paper as he returned to his apartment. He'd forgotten it. His impatience to reach her had made him forget the news. He lighted the lamps in the living room when he reentered. He'd had two drinks, and he didn't want another. He wanted her. He took the paper with him back into the bedroom where he could lounge on the bed, where the phone was close to hand. He turned on the bed light and he looked through the paper until he found the story. It was on an inside page tonight. There was nothing new. The police were still working on the case. That was true. They had valuable leads. That was a lot of eyewash. He read the sports page and the comics, and he rang her again. And again to no avail.

He was beginning to be upset. If she hadn't intended to come home this evening, she could have told him. She'd said she was going for a singing lesson. No singing lesson lasted until this time of night. She knew he was expecting her. She could have called him if she'd been delayed. He tried to look at it reasonably. Honestly tried. She had a lot of friends, of course she did. A girl with her body and hair and strange, lovely face would have more friends than she could handle. He was a newcomer, a nobody in her life. After all, she hadn't met him until yesterday. She couldn't be expected to drop everyone else and devote herself to him alone. She didn't know yet how it was going to be between them. She didn't know it was to be just these two. Two that were one. Until she understood as he did, he couldn't be disturbed that she had other obligations. But she could have told him. She needn't have left him here hanging on the phone, afraid to go out lest it ring. Lying around here without food, smoking too much, reading every line of the damn dull newspaper, waiting for the phone to ring. Wearing out his finger dialing.

The door buzzer sounded with an insolent suddenness while he was still lying there, trying to put down his anger, trying to see it reasonably. He jumped off the bed, and he almost ran to answer. He was angry, yes; he'd tell her plenty, but the heat of it was already dissipated in the eagerness to see her. In the joy of rushing to behold her. He opened the door, and his hand tightened over the knob as he held it wide. Sylvia Nicolai was on the threshold.

"Am I interrupting anything, Dix?" She stood there, tall and slim, at ease, her hands thrust into the deep pockets of her cashmere Burberry, her gilt hair pulled smoothly away from her slender face.

He couldn't believe it, because it wasn't she he expected. It was as if the fire of Laurel had faded, had become polite and cool and ladywise. He recovered himself quickly. He was hearty. "Come in, Sylvia."

"You're quite sure I'm not interrupting you?" She hesitated on the doorstep, looking beyond him into the room as if she expected Laurel there. He knew then, whatever the explanation would be, why Sylvia had come. To get a good look at Laurel.

"Not a bit. I'm not doing a darn thing. Sitting around thinking about dinner and too lazy to start out. I suppose you've eaten?"

She came in, still slightly hesitant. She looked at the room the way a woman looked at a room, sizing it, and approving this one. She loosed her coat with her hands in the pockets, remained standing there on her high-heeled pumps, politely but easily. Like a family friend. Like Brub's wife, who wouldn't want to be an intrusion into a man's privacy. "Oh, yes," she said. "We ate early. We were just starting to Beverly to see a movie when Brub got a call." A slight cloud fleeted over her eyes.

"Not another one?" he asked somberly.

"Oh no." She shook her head hard. As if she couldn't bear to consider that. "Lochner wanted to see him, that was all." She put a smile on her wide, pleasant mouth. "So Brub suggested I run in here and let you amuse me until he could get back. He said it wouldn't take long."

Fleetingly he wondered if it had been Brub's suggestion or if it had been Sylvia's. She had withdrawn from him previously; she didn't now. She was forwarding herself. Her smile at him wasn't reluctant as it had been. It was free. He would have been interested day before yesterday. Now he only feigned it. "I'm delighted, Sylvia. Let me have your coat." She allowed him to help her. She had on a brown sweater and a slim checkered skirt in browns. She was made long and lovely, like a birch tree. Laurel was made lush and warm, like a woman.

She sat down on the couch. "You have a nice place."

"Yes, it is. I was lucky to get it. You'll at least have a drink, won't you?"

"I'll have a Coke. If you have one?"

"I'll join you." He passed her a cigarette, lit it, and left her to get the Cokes. He wondered what Lochner wanted with Brub, important enough to interrupt his evening. He'd find out, for Brub would come here from Lochner. He'd want to talk about it. It was a break. If only they'd be out of here before Laurel returned.

He brought in the Cokes. "Did Brub tell you he and Lochner let me go along today with them?"

"Yes. Thanks." She took the Coke. "How did you like Loch?"

"He seemed bored with it all. Is that his cover-up for being the best bloodhound on the force?"

She said, "He has a wonderful record." Her mouth widened. "As a bloodhound, as you say. He's head of Homicide."

His eyes opened. "He's the head man?" He smiled. "I would never have guessed it."

"That's what Brub says. He seems so different. I've never met him."

"He's worth meeting." Dix relaxed comfortably in the armchair. Head of Homicide. That worried old boy. "A character." He felt easy. "I still can't get used to Brub being a policeman."

"It's funny," Sylvia said seriously. "He always wanted to be one. I suppose lots of little boys did when you and Brub were little boys. Nowadays they want to be jet-propelled pilots, from what I can gather. But Brub never gave up wanting it. And when he asked me if I'd mind, I said I'd be delighted."

"So you're responsible for it," he said with mock solemnity.

"No," she laughed. "But he asked me, and I said I'd be delighted, and I meant it. Anything he wanted, I'd be delighted. It isn't much of a life. Like a doctor, twenty-four hours a day. And you never know when the phone will ring."

"Like tonight."

"Yes." There hadn't been that underlying fear in her until now. It was just a twinge; she'd recovered from the terror that had closed over her Saturday night and yesterday. She could put it away tonight. She could lose it in a bright change of subject. "We saw you last night."

"So Brub told me."

She was to the reason for her visit now. She was eager. "Who was she? The one you were telling us about?"

"Same one. She lives in this house."

"How did you meet her?" She was asking for romance.

He said, "I picked her up."

She made a little face at him.

"As I told Brub, it's the Virginibus Arms' good-neighbor policy," he said. "And high time there was one. It's bad as New York here. There you see your neighbors but don't speak; here you don't even see them."

"You saw her."

"And I picked her up," he said impudently.

"What's her name?"

"Laurel Gray."

"Is she in the movies? She's gorgeous enough to be, from what I saw of her."

"She's done some movies." Again he was struck by how little he knew of her. "She doesn't care much about it. Too early in the mornings for her." He said it with deliberate meaning; she understood.

She said after a moment, "Will you bring her out some evening? We'd like to meet her."

"We'll fix up a date." It was so easy to say, and so easy to avoid doing it. He was feeling better all the time. It had been right that Laurel was delayed. It was in order that she wouldn't have to be inspected by Sylvia. Sylvia wouldn't like Laurel; they weren't cut out of the same goods. Even as he was sure of the rightness, the telephone rang. He excused himself and went to answer, certain it wouldn't be she. It was time for Brub to check back in.

He was so certain it wouldn't be she that he left the bedroom door open. And it was Laurel.

She said, "What are you doing, Dix?"

"Where have you been?" Irritation gnatted him again; she'd stayed out until—after nine o'clock now by the clock. And she turned up asking lightly what he was doing!

"At dinner."

"I thought you were having dinner with me."

"Really? I must have forgotten."

Anger threatened him.

"Why don't you come up?" she asked.

He couldn't. Not now. He said, "I can't."

"Why not?"

"I have company." His anger lurched at Sylvia then for being here, at Brub for sending her here.

There was a sharpness came into her voice. "Who's the girl?"

"What girl?"

"The one on your couch, sweetheart."

She'd seen Sylvia. She must have come to the door, and she'd seen Sylvia and gone away. That explained the insolence in her voice. She was annoyed about it. And again the anger went out of him in the upwelling of emotion; she didn't like his having another woman here.

He couldn't talk openly; the bedroom was too close to the living room. The door open. And Sylvia sitting there silently, listening. Trying not to listen because she was a lady but being unable to miss what he was saying.

"An old friend," he said.

"Business, I presume?" She was sharp.

"As a matter of fact, it is," he agreed.

"In that case, I'll come down."

"No!" He didn't want her to come here. Not until Sylvia and Brub had gone. She must understand. But he couldn't speak out. He spoke as quietly as possible into the mouthpiece. "I'll come up as soon as I'm free."

"What's the matter with my coming down?" she demanded. "Don't you think I'm good enough for your friends?"

He wondered if she'd been drinking. Belligerence wasn't like her—she was slow and sultry and she didn't give a damn for him or anyone. That was in her last night. And tonight, brushing him off for something better or more amusing. Now she was deliberately possessive. There was a reason, and he didn't know the reason. He wanted to shake the hell out of her. She must have known he couldn't talk openly.

"Well?" she demanded.

He said, "I'm busy. I'll see you as soon as I can."

She hung up; the crack smote his eardrum. He was infuriated; he'd wanted to hang up on her, but he hadn't. She'd done it. He went back into the living room scowling, forgetting that he shouldn't scowl, that he wasn't alone.

Sylvia was apologetic. "I am intruding."

"No." He said it flatly. Without explanation. "No." He meant it. He had no objection now to her presence. All anger was transferred to Laurel. The ear she had smote stung sharply. When he saw Sylvia studying his anger, he smiled at her. The smile was hard to come; it pained when it cracked the hard mold of his face. He said, "As a matter of fact, I'm delighted you dropped in, Sylvia. It gives me a feeling of belonging. I think it calls for a celebration— or perhaps a plaque: On this night at this spot Dickson Steele was no more the stranger from the East. After long months, he was at home." He was talking idly, to get that look, that seeking look out of Sylvia's eyes. He wasn't doing half bad.

Most of it was gone when she said, "You've been lonely."

"I expected it." She wasn't trying so hard now. Pity had expelled calculation. He didn't want the pity, and he spoke lightly. "It takes time in a new place. I knew that before I came."

"You could have called on us sooner." It was all gone now, the look and the search.

"Now, would you?" he demanded. "You know how it is. There's always the knowledge that you're making a forced entry into the other fellow's life. Sometimes friendship survives it. More often it only spoils a good memory."

"It's worth trying," she said. "How else can—"

The doorbell rang. Brub, and it hadn't taken long. The business with Loch couldn't have been too important. He went to the door talking, breaking in on Sylvia's words. Wanting Brub to see how ordinary this had been. "Sometimes the dissent isn't mutual, Sylvia. The fellow who closes the door feels a hell of a lot worse than the eager beaver. I wouldn't want to be—"

Laurel stood there. Because she had been angry, because she had hung up on him in anger, he was so amazed that his words didn't dissipate; they became an utter void. He didn't realize he was scowling at her until she mirrored it ludicrously. "And what did the big bad wolf say then to Little Red Riding Hood, darling?" Deliberately she stepped past him and went into the room while he stood there scowling and empty-mouthed.

They were together, Sylvia and Laurel. Each had come for that reason, to look upon the other. He didn't know exactly why it mattered to either of them. He wasn't a sweepstake. Sylvia didn't care at all; Laurel cared little enough. They were eyeing each other in the faint patronizing manner of all women to women, no matter the stake, when he turned into the living room.

He'd had a slight apprehension over the phone that Laurel might have been drinking. She hadn't been. Her scent was perfumed, not alcoholic; she had never looked more glowing. She was in white, all white but for her radiant hair and painted mouth and eyes. Before her Sylvia was colorless and yet before Sylvia, Laurel was too richly colored. Between them was the gulf of a circumstance of birth and a pattern of living.

He said, "Sylvia, this is Laurel." And to Laurel, "This is Sylvia. My friend Brub Nicolai's wife."

They acknowledged the introduction in monotone, in the same manner of social courtesy, but it did not diminish the gulf. There was nothing could diminish the gulf.

He said, "Let me take your coat, Laurel. Drink?"

"No, thanks. I've just had dinner." Her eyes were strange amber flowers. She opened them full on him. "I've been trying to call you for hours. Where have you been?"

She was a dirty little liar. She was trying to tell Sylvia it hadn't been she on the phone getting the brush-off. He looked at Sylvia and his mouth quirked. She wasn't fooling Sylvia. You didn't fool Sylvia. She burrowed under words, under the way of a face and a smile for the actuality. He was suddenly cold. For he knew, was certain of the fact, that Sylvia had been burrowing beneath his surface since the night he had come out of the fog into her existence. Irritation heated him. She had no business trying to find an under self in him; she should have taken him as he was taken, an average young fellow, pleasant company; beyond that, her husband's old friend. It couldn't have been Brub who set her on him. There could have been no suspicion when he came to Brub's house that night. Nor was there; yet Sylvia had searched his face and the way he spoke—and she hadn't liked him.

He knew it with cold clarity. He'd sensed it from the first moment of meeting: she didn't like him. He didn't like her either with her damn prying mind. Her bitching, high-toned mind. Brub was all right; she wasn't going to spoil Brub with Dix. She wasn't going to be allowed.

He said to Laurel, "I've been right here since five o'clock." He lit her cigarette. "Maybe you had the wrong number."

"Maybe I did." She took her eyes from him and laid them again on Sylvia. She didn't think any more of Sylvia than Sylvia of her. She was more open about it, that was the way of her, the way that couldn't be helped. Yet she had a fear of Sylvia that had no echo in Brub's wife. She was harder than Sylvia could ever be, but she wasn't fine steel; she could be broken. She said to Sylvia, and the smear of insolence was under the surface, "Where's your husband?" She let it rest until Sylvia was ready to answer, and then she didn't wait for the answer. "I've wanted to meet him. I've heard so much about him."

A dirty little liar. He'd not told her much or little of Brub. Brub's name hadn't been spoken between them.

Sylvia said, "He'll be along. He had some business, and I decided Dix would be more amusing than business." She gave him a woman smile. Not for him, for Laurel because she scorned Laurel.

"And Dix wasn't," Dix said, waiting for her disavowal.

She was provocative as Laurel would have been. "I don't know," she said.

"Is your husband on the Mildred Atkinson thing?" Laurel asked abruptly.

He hadn't thought she knew who Brub Nicolai was, but she had known. And she'd brought up from the shadows that which Sylvia and Dix had been pretending didn't exist there. She didn't care; all she was attempting was destruction of their mood. Succeeding better than she could know.

"Yes, he's working on it." Sylvia didn't like the mention of the case. That quickly the tightness was in her fingers, the set of her lips. She didn't dissemble well.

"Gorgon told me he was," Laurel nodded. She didn't explain Gorgon, nor did Sylvia. But Sylvia knew the name; she admitted knowledge by accepting Gorgon as casually as he was offered. Laurel went on, "He was talking about it tonight. He says Brub Nicolai's the smartest young dick in the department."

He felt Sylvia's cringe at Laurel's use of the word dick for detective. He didn't see it; he saw nothing. His mind was knotted too tightly, so tightly the room was a blur. He steadied himself against the table.

It was good that Sylvia was there; that he was not alone with Laurel. She had been out with someone named Gorgon while Dix waited here for her. The desperate need to be alone with Laurel, to force truth from her, began hammering against his temples until he wanted to cry out from the pain of it. He had to stand there, holding himself by the pressure of his palms on the table, while the two made conversation about Brub, Brub who should be here and take his wife away.

He had to stand braced there listening to Laurel quote Gorgon to Sylvia, all of Gorgon's damn omniscience about Brub Nicolai's growing prowess as a detective.

He couldn't have endured much longer. The door buzzer reprieved him. He left the two women without excusing himself. They didn't know he was there. It was Brub at last; the Brub of these days, a frown between his eyebrows, a distant look on his face until he saw Dix and smiled.

"Hello. Sylvia still here?"

"Yeah. We've been gabbing. Come on in." He let Brub precede him into the living room. He didn't want to hear any more about Gorgon. He didn't have to. By the time he rounded into the room, Sylvia was making introductions.

"Brub, this is Laurel Gray. My husband, Mr. Nicolai."

Laurel's eyes took stock of Brub in the same way they had taken stock of Dix on first meeting. Thoroughly, boldly, despite Sylvia's presence. It might be Laurel knew no better, it might be unconscious. The only way she knew to look at a man. Sylvia watched, but she wasn't disturbed. Not about Laurel. Only when Brub had acknowledged the introduction and turned to his wife did the waver of fear come to her.

Her voice was controlled, but the fear cooled it. "Everything . . . all right, darling?"

He nodded; his smile reassured her. But it wasn't real. It came and it went. As brief as a flicker of light in the darkness.

Dix said heartily, "How about a drink, Brub?"

"Thanks." The response was automatic, without thought, for with thought Brub shook his head. "But not tonight." As if that had been what he meant to say in the first place. "I'm too tired. Ready, Sylvia?"

"Yes." She spoke brightly as if unaware of Brub's depression.

Dix didn't attempt to delay them. He knew Brub had information on the case to impart; he knew Brub would talk if he remained for a drink. The case wasn't important to Dix at the moment; he wanted one thing only, to be alone with Laurel.

He only said, "Sorry," putting real feeling into it, as real as if it were honest. "You better take it easy a few days. You do look tired. Can't you fence him in, Sylvia?"

"I wish I could." But she too was acting. Her thoughts were on Brub only.

She and Laurel said the false and polite things required. Brub nodded; he was in a hurry to be gone. His arm held Sylvia's closely.

"I'll give you a ring," Dix promised. He held the door ajar until they had crossed the patio, until they walked under the arch to the street. He closed it then, definitely. One stride carried him to the entrance to the living room.

Laurel coiled in the chair, her eyes smoldering, her mouth insolent, ready to strike.

He struck first. "Who is Gorgon?"

She didn't answer him. "What's the idea of that woman here?" she demanded.

He repeated, "Who is Gorgon?"

"Giving me the runaround, telling me not to come down here. Business!" Her voice spat.

He only repeated, "Who is Gorgon?" He began to move towards her then. There was no sound of him crossing the room.

There was no sound but her voice berating, "You can't play me that way. There isn't any man I'll take that from. God knows, I won't take it from you."

He was standing over her. "Who is Gorgon?" The knots in his head were tightening. He couldn't stand the tightness. His hands reached down, clamped on her shoulders, and he pulled her out of the chair. "Who—"

She spoke with cold nastiness. "If you don't take your hands off me, you won't be any good to any woman anymore." Through her shoulders, he felt the shift of her weight, and he released her, stepped away quickly. She had meant the words. The knots loosened as quickly, the shock of her intent was as ice flung in his face. With the diminishing of pain, he was weakened, his forehead was wet. He drew his sleeve across it, across the dampness of his eyes.

He heard her say, "I'm getting to hell out of here."

He couldn't have stopped her, weakened as he was. His voice was husky. "Don't go."

He didn't even look at her. He didn't know why she didn't leave; curiosity, perhaps. It couldn't have been pity; she wasn't a woman to have pity on a man.

He was surprised at the sound of her voice; it wasn't hating now. It shrugged. "I think we both need a drink."

He heard her go to the kitchen, and he flung himself facedown on the couch, his fingers gripped tight into his palms. He had wanted to kill her.

When he heard the sound of her returning, he turned. She was standing over him, and she held out the glass. "Thanks, Laurel."

She went back to the chair, sat down, and drank.

He took a swallow from his glass, another. She'd mixed it strong.

"Feel better?" she asked.

"Yes. I needed this."

"Shall we start all over?"

His eyes went quickly to her. She meant it. He was ashamed of his anger; it hadn't been he; some stranger had performed that way. But the stranger was himself.

"Let's do."

"You want to know who Gorgon is. He's my lawyer."

He was more ashamed. He didn't say anything.

"I ran into him when I was leaving the studio. He wanted to talk over some business. It was nearly six." Her eyes hardened. "I figured it wouldn't hurt him to buy me a meal." She looked away. "I couldn't call you, Dix. I didn't want him—snooping."

It was all explained. Warmth filled him, good and tender warmth. She'd wanted to be with him, to run back to him. Wanted it as much as he. He hadn't been wrong; they were meant to coexist. He was ready to rush to her when she hardened again. "What about her?"

He laughed. "It's as dull as yours. Brub dropped her off while he went on business. I didn't want her here."

Her words barbed. "Then why did you try to keep me away? Didn't you think I was good enough to meet her?"

"Good God, Laurel!" He was exasperated, the more so because she wasn't up to Sylvia's par. Yet she soared above Sylvia.

"Didn't you?" she demanded.

He wasn't going to get angry again. He wouldn't let her make him angry. "Listen," he said, "I didn't want you let in on something that would bore the tar out of you. That's point one. Two, I was sore at you for not showing up."

"You expected me?"

"You know damn well I expected you. We were going to have dinner together—"

"Three?"

**108**

She was pleased, there was an up curve of her rich mouth, the mockery was again in her golden eyes.

"Three, I wanted you alone, for myself, all alone, not cluttered up with a lot of dumb people." His voice wasn't steady, nor was he as he pushed up to his feet. Yet he could move, and he went to her, pulling her again out of the chair. His hands were strong this time, not cruel.

She said, "Wait a minute, Dix." Her palms pushed against his shoulders, her body twisted, but he didn't let her go. His mouth closed over hers, and he held her until she quieted. He held her for a long time.

When he released her, there was laughter in him where there had been pain. Exultant laughter. He said, "That's the way it is, Laurel. That's the way it has to be. You—and me."

She was as beautiful as if set aflame. Her eyes slanted up at him, even her eyes were aflame. She pushed back her hair. "I guess you're right," she said. She rubbed at her arm. "But don't try the rough stuff again. I won't take it."

"I'm sorry." He was, and for a moment he tightened. He was more than sorry. He was afraid. He might have hurt her. He might have lost her. With her he must remember, he must never take a chance of losing her. If it had happened he shook his head and a tremble went over him.

She said anxiously, "What's the matter?"

He didn't answer, he took her into his arms and held her: held her without explanation until he was quieted again.

# 2

IT WAS morning, and the sun lay bright blue against the open window. And the sun lay mildly gold where her hair had flamed on the white pillow, where again her head would rest. The room was swirling with sun, and he rested there content in brightness. It was good to wake to sun, to warmth, and remembrance of warmth and bright beauty. It was good to know she would return after her little errands and business appointments and lessons were done, would return eagerly to his eagerness. For him there were the hours of day to pass, but they would trickle through his hands as quietly, as simply as sand. The sun and the day would pass; there would come night. And the night would flame with a radiance surpassing the sun.

The day passed and there was the night and another day and another night and another. Until he did not know the count of the hours or of the days. Or of the nights. They were one unto the other, a circle whirling evenly, effortlessly, endlessly. He knew beauty and the intensity of a dream, and he was meshed in a womb he called happiness. He did not think: this must come to an end in time. A circle had no beginning or end; it existed. He did not allow thought to enter the hours that he waited for her, laved in memory of her presence. He seldom left the apartment in those days. In the outside world there was time; in time, there was impatience. Better to remain within the dream. Even the broom-and-mop harridan could little disturb the dream.

He did not say: this will not endure forever. He did not face the awakening. There was the morning when the fleet of clouds passed over the sun, but he did not accept the augury. He did not admit to mind the chill that came through the windows of an afternoon even as he closed the windows. He did not admit the scrim of gray shutting away the stars on that night.

He knew, but he did not admit. It might have been a week, it might have been a day or two, or perhaps there was no time. But the restlessness was coming into her. She could not be content too long to be bound within the confines of this dream. It might have been the way her shoulders moved to a dance orchestra over the radio. It might have been the small frown as they sat again for dinner in the living room. It could have been her evasion to his questions about her hours of that particular day. Or the way in which she stood at the doorway, looking out into the night.

He had known from the beginning she was meant to be displayed. She could not be hidden away long in the cave of his dream. Yet he could not admit. She had to be the one to speak.

She telephoned him. Late, five o'clock or later. She said, "Dix, I can't meet you for dinner tonight. . . . It's business."

He knew a little more about her now, not much, a little. She didn't talk of herself, no more than did he. There had been slight need of words within the cave. But he knew she was studying and waiting for the big chance. Her sights were high; others had been discovered by the magical screen. She intended to be. Talent wasn't of the same import as knowing the right guardians of the portal. The philosopher's stone was contacts.

He couldn't let her know his disappointment. They hadn't played it that way. They hadn't been soft lovers; they'd been aware of worldly needs. He wouldn't have dared let her know his adolescent urgency. He said, "Sorry," as if it didn't matter. "See you later?"

He could sense her hesitation.

"If I'm not too late. There's a party after." There was definite hesitation now, if slight. "I'm to sing."

He knew better, but he demanded, "No matter how late, come. Wake me up."

She didn't say yes or no; she said nothing in a rush of words. After she had rung off, it began. Slowly at first. Like fog wisping into his mind. Only a small doubt. He could, at first, brush it away. But it moved in thicker; tightening around the coils of his brain, blotting out reason.

She was with another man. Someone with money to spend on her, big money. Uncle Fergus! Dix almost ran to the desk. He hadn't looked at mail during these days, once or twice maybe he'd riffled for a Princeton postmark, not finding it, finding nothing but bills for Mel Terriss. Then he had forgotten mail, forgotten the dunning bills, forgotten everything in her. He pawed through the neat stack of envelopes and he found it, the letter from Uncle Fergus. There was a check inside. He glanced at the figures, two hundred and fifty dollars. He pushed open the brief typewritten letter. It said:

> Dear Dickson,
>
> If you have a bad back and are not just inventing same to get out of work, I suggest you apply to the Veterans' Hospital for treatment. As for my sending you additional funds, the idea is as stupid as yours usually . . .

He crumpled the letter into a tight angry ball and hurled it across the room. He didn't even finish reading it. He knew too well the pious platitudes about work and pay; he'd heard them all his life. When other fellows had cars and clothes and free spending, he had platitudes. It wasn't that the old skinflint didn't have it. There was plenty of money for stocks and bonds, real estate. Everything salted away for an old man's idea about being a solid citizen. You'd think Uncle Fergus would have recognized the need for the things that made living worth living. He'd been a poor clod, son of a dirt farmer. He'd never had anything either, starting to work in a Princeton hardware store when he was fourteen (how well Dickson knew every step of Uncle Fergus's meager life; he could recite it like a nursery rhyme), studying nights to get himself into the university. Dickson could see him, one of those poor boobs, peasants, owning one dark, ill-fitting suit and a pair of heavy-soled shoes, clumping to class, study, and work, and nobody knew he was in Princeton but the other peasants. Not even coming out of it cum laude, the needed touch for a big success story. Nothing, just grubbing through, worrying along to graduation; getting nothing but a diploma and a fixed belief that to be a Princeton man was like being a senator or maybe Jehovah.

Dix hadn't wanted to be a Princeton man. Not that kind. If it could have been right, if he could have been one of the fellows he saw around town, driving a fast car, careless about expensive clothes and money and girls, club fellows, he'd have grabbed it. He might as well have wanted to be senator or the Jehovah. He was Fergus Steele's nephew, and he worked in the hardware store after hours all through high school. Either he worked or he had nothing to spend. That was Uncle Fergus's hand-embroidered, gold-framed motto: No work, no money.

A fellow had to have money. You couldn't get a girl without money in your pockets. A girl didn't notice your looks or your sharp personality, not unless you could take her to the movies or the Saturday night dance. And feed her after the show.

Dix hadn't learned then how to get money without working for it. Except maybe filching a dime or a quarter from the cash register now and again. Lying about it. Once he took five dollars; he needed it too. You couldn't take a girl to the Junior Prom without sending her flowers. Uncle Fergus fired a delivery boy for that one.

Dix knew damn well he'd go through hell at the university. He did. He suffered, God how he suffered, that first year. He'd have quit, he'd have flunked out quick, but the alternative was far worse: being packed off like a piece of cattle to a farm Uncle Fergus owned in western Pennsylvania. Either he had to be a gentleman, according to Uncle Fergus's standards, or he could revert to the peasantry. Dix was smart enough to know he couldn't get a job, stand on his own feet. He didn't want to work that hard. He took the first year, working in the hardware store after school, afraid to look anyone in the eye, afraid he'd see the sneers openly, or the pity.

It was along in the spring that he started getting wise. Latching on to boys with money, rich stinkers who hadn't any better place in the university scheme than Dix himself. They really were stinkers; Mel Terriss was a good example of the breed. But they had money. They were good for a tip if you knew a place to get a bottle of booze after hours, or took their cars to be serviced, or picked up their cleaning. They were good for a cash loan in return for a hard-luck story. You could wear their clothes, smoke their cigarettes, drink their liquor. As long as you toadied, you had a pretty good life. It notched them up higher if they could sneer at a boob of a townsman who had less than they. He took the sneers with the tips, and the second year wasn't so bad.

The second year he found Mel Terriss, who hadn't even made the stinkers' set. He got Mel into the circle, and he saw that Mel repaid him. It was easy sailing for Dix after that, with Mel's clothes and Mel's car and the babes thinking Dix was the rich guy and Mel the stooge. Dix had the looks and the air; he had everything Mel needed. Mel was kept soothed by Dix bringing him the women that Dix couldn't be bothered with. And by booze. Mel was headed straight for alcoholism even then, a kid in college. The booze made him believe he was what he alone thought he was, not a stinker. Only it made him a worse stinker, of course. End of the term, Dix was Mel's only friend. That suited Dix. It looked like two good years ahead if he could keep Mel in college; so far he'd showed Mel how to manage it with Mel's money, paying grubs to tutor Mel through. He and Mel hated each other's guts, but each without the other was lost. They stuck together.

That was the summer when the young men knew war was fact. The only question was when it would be acknowledged. And that summer Dix enlisted in the Air Corps. All the top men of the campus were enlisting.

The war years were the first happy years he'd ever known. You didn't have to kowtow to the stinking rich. You were all equal in pay; and before long, you were the rich guy. Because you didn't give a damn and you were the best God-damned pilot in the company with promotions coming fast. You wore swell tailored uniforms, high polish on your shoes. You didn't need a car. You had something better, sleek powerful planes. You were the Mister; you were what you'd always wanted to be, class. You could have any woman you wanted in Africa or India or England or Australia or the United States, or any place in the world. The world was yours.

That life was so real that there wasn't any other life. Even when the war was over, there was no realization of another life. Not until he stood again in the small, dark living room of his uncle's home. It came as shock, the return to Uncle Fergus; he hadn't really known it wasn't going to be always the way it had been in the war years. He had mistaken interlude for life span.

Uncle Fergus had done well for himself too during the war years. He'd invented some kind of nail or screw or tool and manufactured it. But getting richer hadn't made a change in the old man. He lived the way he always had lived, in the same uncomfortable house, with the same slovenly old housekeeper, the same badly cooked meals, and bad lighting. The only difference was more stocks and bonds and real estate. It was in a bathos of patriotism that Uncle Fergus consented to Dix's year in California to write a book. Oh, Dix had had to do some fast talk. The old skinflint thought he was living with friends who could help him, who would keep him in line. He explained the frequent change of address as difficulties in getting office space. Once the offer was made, Uncle Fergus regretted his generosity; that was obvious. But it was too late. Dix didn't let him withdraw.

In excess of anger Dix took the measly check now and tore it into little pieces, tore it and retore it and scattered it all over Mel's rug. The usual check, the pittance on which to exist another month. Go to a Veterans' Hospital. Beg—you're a veteran, aren't you?

He sat there at the desk, holding his hot head with his steeled fingers. Seeing through his fingers the stack of bills addressed to Mel Terriss. It was rotten luck running into Mel that night. Why couldn't he have met Mel during the war years, when he could have sneered down at him the way he'd wanted to all his life? But Mel had been hiding out in some factory; even the Army hadn't wanted Mel. When they met, the war was long over and Mel was a rich stinker again.

Dix had tried not to speak to Mel in the bar that night. He'd avoided the recognition, forgetting you couldn't avoid an ass like Mel. Mel had to weave over and poke his fat, stupid face across the table. Dix could see what was churning in Mel's mind as he looked at the blonde. Ready to start over the same old way, let Dix do the dirty work, procure the girls in exchange for tips. Well, it hadn't worked that way; he'd stopped bootlicking six years ago. And maybe it wasn't so bad running into Mel. Dix had the apartment and the car and the clothes; the charge accounts wouldn't hold out forever, but they were still good enough. That was the sort of money Mel had. And Mel was in Rio, good old Mel!

Without Mel, there would have been no Laurel. His brain cooling, the hunger for Laurel began gnawing again. Maybe she had had a chance to sing at some big event; she wouldn't turn it down, he knew that, even if she hungered for him as he for her. She was like him that way. She was after big time. The only difference was she wasn't looking for money; she wanted a spotlight.

Hatred of Uncle Fergus surged anew. Unless Dix could help Laurel get that spotlight, he'd be sloughed. As soon as the new wore off him. As soon as she found out he was broke. He couldn't lose her; she was the only thing he had, the only right thing he'd had since he took off his uniform. In shame he got down on his hands and knees and began gathering up the tiny pieces of the check. He had to have this much money; it wouldn't last long, but it would prolong things for another week. Maybe by that time he could raise more. There must be ways to get gravy out here; there were sure to be, only he hadn't been looking for them. He hadn't needed to, the two-fifty did well enough before he met Laurel. Delicately he picked up each small piece, being careful not to crumple them. And then came the fear that Laurel would return suddenly, find him in this ridiculous position. He began to work faster, nervously. When he had retrieved all the scraps, his hands were wet and shaking. He had to wipe the palms on his shirt before he dared piece the check together. He was careful despite his shaking fingers, putting each small piece in its proper place. Until they were put together and one piece missing. It had to be a piece of value, the "Fergu" of the signature. Frantically he searched for it, crawling on the floor like a baby, trembling with the fear that she or someone would come before it was found.

He spied it finally, under the desk chair. He had the check again! He didn't know if a bank would accept it, whether it would be necessary to write again to Uncle Fergus with some excuse about its destruction. The maid mixing it with advertising folders, tearing it up. Uncle Fergus wouldn't believe his story. He'd stop payment on the first check and then he'd wait to make sure it hadn't been cashed before he sent a second. It would be a month at least before Uncle Fergus would return a check to Dix, a month with not more than a ten spot left in his pocket.

Worrying about what could happen, a sickness came over him, so real that he felt weak as a cat. He could scarcely make it to the couch. He flopped there, his eyes closed, his fingers tight in his palms. He couldn't lose Laurel. He wouldn't lose her. No matter what he did. He could go to work. There must be plenty of jobs. Laurel knew a lot of rich people; maybe he could give her a story about needing to get into something. Not for money. For research. Or Brub. Brub might get him on the police force.

He could smile at that; and he then felt better. Only what would Laurel be doing while Dix was on call twenty-four hours a day? She wouldn't be sitting at home; she wasn't a Sylvia.

He couldn't go to work; there were other ways of getting money. If Laurel would only introduce him to some of her friends; the easiest way to get money was through those who had money. He knew how to do it that way. Why was Laurel keeping him hidden? Anger was rising; he mustn't get angry now. He couldn't take another spasm. He went to the bar, and he poured a heavy slug of the stuff; he didn't want it, but it settled his stomach.

If he knew where Laurel was, he'd go to her now. If she cared anything about him, she'd have wanted him there tonight to hear her sing. He didn't believe she was singing. She had another man; whenever she got a chance to be with that man, she didn't care whom she knocked down.

He couldn't remain here all evening thinking these thoughts, suffering these agonies. He'd go nuts. He had to get out, go where he could breathe. Go hide himself in the night.

He caught his breath. He didn't dare. It was too soon. The police were still on the alert. And there was Laurel. He didn't dare do anything that might spoil what he had with Laurel. But he couldn't stay here. He had to get away from thinking his thoughts.

He went to the bedroom, seized the telephone. He didn't know how many times Brub had called during these days, these weeks. Dix had abruptly turned down all advances. But he'd left the door open. When the surge of work was over, he'd call Brub. He didn't notice the time until after he'd dialed; he was relieved to see that it wasn't late at all, not quite nine o'clock.

It was Sylvia who answered. She sounded not only surprised to hear from him but almost as if she'd never before heard his voice. He asked for Brub. "Is he home? Thought I might run out for a little if he isn't busy."

By that time she seemed to know him again. She was cordial. "Do come out. We've been wondering when you'd get your nose out of that book."

"Sure you don't mind?"

"We welcome you," she said quickly. "And I do mean it. Brub was so bored just sitting around with me, he's gone next door to borrow a rake or a deck of cards or something."

"He isn't at home?"

"He will be before you get here," she said with certainty. "Come along."

He felt better right away. He felt himself again. Sure of himself, happy, easy. He'd stayed in too closely with Laurel; that wasn't good for a man. Maybe she'd felt it too. Maybe that was why she'd taken this job tonight. But she couldn't have felt too shut in; she'd been out every day on lessons or beauty appointments or some excuse.

He didn't bother to change his clothes. He grabbed the nearest jacket, putting it on as he returned to the living room. He had to delay there. The torn check was on the desk. He wouldn't want Laurel to see it. He scooped the pieces into an envelope, sealed it to make certain he wouldn't lose any precious bit, and stuck it in his jacket pocket. He looked down at the stack of bills addressed to Mel, wondering if Laurel had noticed them, and if she had, why she hadn't said anything. Someone had stacked them in that neat pile, not he. It could have been the slattern, but it could have been Laurel. It probably had been Laurel; he could see her hands now arranging the paper and the magazines on the table. Idly, deliberately. She could have done the same to the mail while he was dressing or putting on the coffee. Idly, but she would have noticed. Noticed and wondered. He swept the mail into the drawer, banging it shut. He wasn't going to think in circles; he was going to Brub's and forget.

# 3

HE LEFT the apartment by the back door. It gave him a good feeling as soon as he stepped into the night; he was doing something familiar. The night too was good; there were no stars, only hazy darkness. He went softly through the alley to the garage. The sound of the door opening couldn't carry back to the apartments. The hinges were well oiled.

The car looked good. He hadn't had it out for days, and it felt good to be at the wheel. He didn't have to back out quietly, he let it purr; he was going to visit his friend, his friend the policeman.

By the time he reached the Nicolais' there was no anger, no tension left in him. He whistled his way up the walk. Brub opened the door, and things were good again, the way they'd been that first night. Brub in sneakers and a pair of pants as wrinkled as his own. Holding out his hand saying, "You're a sight for sore eyes. What's the idea of the brush-off, genius?"

It was all good until they came into the living room together, as they had on that first night. And as on the first night, Sylvia was there. Filling the room, for all her quietness. Fading out the bright colors for all the monotone of her silver-gray slack suit, her pale gold hair, her pale, serious face. There was no welcome in her eyes for him. She was looking at him as at a stranger. In an instant she smiled, but the smile was a pale thing, and in her eyes there was no smile. He felt himself an intruder and he was angry; if she hadn't wanted him to come here tonight, she could have said so; she could have said Brub was out and let it go at that. But she'd urged him to come; she'd even called Brub home for his coming.

When she spoke, it was better. "Finished that book?" she asked as if they'd been together daily. "I'm dying to read it." Yet in the midst of her words, she chilled again. And recovered, giving him a wider smile. "How about a beer?"

"Let me," Dix said, but she was already up from the chair, crying, "I'm the official beer getter around here. You sit down." She wasn't smooth and polished in her motions tonight; there was a nervousness as she went to the bar. Maybe she and Brub had had a scrap; maybe that was why he'd gone to the neighbors, and why she'd urged Dix to come, to get them past the awkward stage. At any rate there was no difference in Brub, good old Brub, reclining himself on the couch and saying, "I was afraid you'd skipped back East, Dix."

"Just work," he answered. He sounded like anyone who worked, regretful of the time it took, almost apologetic.

"Finished?"

"God, no!" He laughed easily. "But the heat was off, so I decided a break was in order." Sylvia set the glass and bottle at hand on the end table. Dix took the opposite side of the couch, pushing Brub's sneakers aside. He smiled up at Sylvia. "That's why I barged in on you. Hope I'm not in the way."

"Not at all! I told you we were bored, didn't I?" She looked down at Brub. "Beer, darling?"

"Might as well."

But there wasn't the smilingness between them as on that first night, not the ease and two-is-one perfection. Something was wrong. Dix didn't care about their troubles. He'd needed a quiet evening like this, with beer and Brub gabbing about his boat. Brub was a kid about boats. Dix didn't want to talk; he wanted only to be lulled by this kind of aimless conversation.

There was no mention of the case; there was no case until Dix mentioned it. Until he said, "How's the case coming?"

Under his eyes he watched Sylvia, awaited her reaction. He was disappointed. There wasn't a reaction tonight. She was too quiet, too colorless to be more quiet or of less color. There was no change in her at all.

"Nothing new," Brub answered. "It's stymied. Same as the others. No clues, no fresh evidence, no hints."

Brub wasn't lying to him. Brub was disgusted, but he wasn't discouraged as he had been before. The life had gone out of the case. It wasn't closed because the police didn't close the books, but it was as good as closed. Brub even switched the subject. "Remember Ad Tyne, Dix?"

He didn't.

Brub insisted, "Sure you do. Adam Tyne. The flight commander from Bath. Nice quiet fellow. We saw a lot of him that spring of forty-three. The blond one."

He searched for memory, but he didn't find Adam Tyne. There'd been a lot of good fellows; Adam Tyne could have been any of them. Not that it was important. Brub was continuing, "Had a letter from him the first of the week. I wrote him when I got back but hadn't heard a thing. He's married, settled down. Wish I had the letter here, darn it, but I left it at the office." Brub's voice changed, became grave. The transition was so sudden that there was no time to attune to the change before the words were spoken. "He had a sad piece of news. Brucie is dead."

*Brucie is dead.* The words quivered in the vacuum of quietness. *Brucie is dead.* They resounded thunderously in the silence. *Brucie is dead.*

When he could, he began to echo them as he should, with proper shock, with the right incredulity. "Brucie is—" He couldn't finish above a whisper. His voice broke, "—dead." The tears were rolling down his cheeks; he covered his face, tried to withhold the sobs that were clawing him. *Brucie is dead.* The words had never been spoken before. He had not known what would happen when they were spoken.

He heard from a far-off place Sylvia's little, hurt cry, "Dix!"

He heard Brub's embarrassed apology, "Dix, I didn't know—"

He couldn't answer them. He couldn't stop crying. It was a long time before he could stop; it seemed eternity within the confines of the shocked silence. He lifted his head when he could and said huskily, "I'm sorry." It released Sylvia and Brub. They didn't know the agony raking his heart.

"I didn't know," Brub said again. He blew his nose loudly. "I didn't know you—and Brucie—"

He said simply, "She meant everything in the world to me." *Brucie*, his soul wept; *Brucie*. He took out his handkerchief and blew his nose. Sylvia's eyes were large as moons, pale moons, sad. "We didn't know," she whispered.

"No," he shook his head. "I guess no one knew. It was all over." He put the handkerchief away. He could talk all right now; they didn't know anything he was thinking. "How did she die? Buzz bombs?"

Brub said, "She was murdered."

He could show shock because he was shocked. He had never expected to hear it said. It was so long ago. He echoed, "Murdered."

Brub nodded. His face looked as if it hurt.

Dix had to ask. Painfully, as it should be asked by a man who'd loved her. "How did it—what happened—who did it?"

Brub said, "The police have never found out." He blew his nose again. "Better not talk about it, Dix."

His jaw was firm. "I want to know." His eyes promised that he could take it.

"She was down for a weekend at a small beach place. Her husband was coming to join her. At least that's what she told the landlady." Brub told it with starts and stops; he didn't want to tell it. Dix was forcing him to tell it. "Her husband didn't come. Or if he did, no one saw him. She went out Saturday evening alone; she didn't come back. She wasn't found for several weeks. In a rocky cove—she'd been strangled."

Dix couldn't speak. He could only look at Brub out of unseeing eyes.

"It was some time before she was identified. She hadn't signed the register under her own name." Brub said almost apologetically, "I wouldn't have dreamed she was that kind of a girl. She was always gay—but she was so—so nice—you know, like a girl from home."

"She wasn't that kind," Dix choked. "She wasn't."

Sylvia wanted to say something, but she didn't. She just sat there like a ghost with her sad, luminous eyes on Dix. He knew he had to get out, before he broke down again. He didn't know how to leave.

"They never found any trace of the husband. It must have happened just after our outfit left England. That's why we didn't know, why we never heard about it." And he said what was true. "There'd been so much killing, one more wasn't news."

Brucie had died but no one cared, only he. All of them had lost so many, dear as brothers, as their own selves, they had learned not to talk about death. They had refused to think about death being death. Even in the heart's inmost core where each dwelled alone, they did not admit death.

Dix said unsteadily, "I'd better go." He tried to smile at them. "Sorry."

They tried to stop him. They wanted him to stay and forget in their sympathy and their understanding, in their love for him at this moment. He couldn't stay. He had to get out, to be alone in his lonely place. To remember and to forget. He brushed aside their urging the way you brushed away smoke; knowing it would recur but you could again brush it away. He went into the night while they stood close to each other in the doorway. Together. Never alone.

He drove away not knowing where he was going or why. Only to get away. He did not know how far he drove or how long.

There was no thinking in his mind; there was only sound, the swish of the dark wet water over the cold sand, colder than Brucie; the water was the voice of a girl, a voice hushed by fear, repeating over and over *No . . . no . . . no . . .* Fear wasn't a jagged split of light cleaving you; fear wasn't a cold fist in your entrails; fear wasn't something you could face and demolish with your arrogance. Fear was the fog, creeping about you, winding its tendrils about you, seeping into your pores and flesh and bone. Fear was a girl whispering a word over and again, a small word you refused to hear although the whisper was a scream in your ears, a dreadful scream you could never forget. You heard it over and again and the fog was a ripe red veil you could not tear away from your eyes. Brucie was dead. Brucie whom he had loved, who was his only love.

She had loved him! If there hadn't been a marriage, one of those secret war marriages. Only she couldn't see it was unimportant; she loved Dix, but she loved that unknown husband too. She didn't know the unknown one would die so soon. Somewhere over Germany. So many died. She was all mixed up; she wasn't bad. She was good! He didn't know until she died how good she was. She hadn't done anything wrong; it wasn't wrong to love. When you were filled with love, overflowing with love, you had to give love. If it weren't for that boy who was to die over Germany. If Dix had only known. The swish of the waves whispering *If . . . if . . . if . . .* And Brucie dead. Little Brucie.

How long, how far he drove, he didn't know. With his fingers clenching the wheel and the waves crashing in his ears. He didn't once stop the car. He drove until emotional exhaustion left him empty as a gourd. Until no tears, no rage, no pity had meaning for him. At some point he turned the car to home. He had no memory of the act until he reached his garage, rolled the car into it. He was so tired he walked like one drugged, dragging his leaden body through the dark alley to the dark apartment. He went in through the kitchen, pushing one heavy foot after the other. It wasn't until he entered the bedroom and saw her that he remembered the existence of Laurel. Until he remembered with agonized relief that he was no longer alone.

She must have heard him coming, for she'd turned on the bed-side lamp and she was standing by the bed holding the yellow chiffon of her negligee tightly about her. Even in his exhaustion he realized the fear on her face. It was gone before the realization.

"I didn't know it was you," she said, then her voice sharpened. "Where have you been all night?"

He was too weary to answer questions, to ask them. He stumbled to her. She couldn't back away more than a step, the table halted her. He put his arms around her and he held her, holding her warmth and the life that flowed beneath her flesh. He held her and he said, "Help me. I'm tired—so tired."

# 4

IT WAS afternoon before he awoke. There was no sun on the windows. Outside was grayness; the sky was watered gray silk.

He wasn't rested. He was heavy, tired, although his sleep had been dreamless. He took a cigarette from his pack on the bed table, lighted it. He wondered where Laurel was. Without her last night, or this morning, he wouldn't have dared sleep, fearing the dream. She had known; she hadn't asked questions after that first one. She had given comfort, helping him undress, laying back the covers, laying herself and her warmth beside him, within his arms.

He ought to get up, not lie here in the comfort of bed. Shower, shave, dress before she returned. She'd come back as soon as she'd finished her business. She wouldn't call; she'd come. She knew he needed her. She had cared for him last night. Laying back the covers . . .

She hadn't been to bed! She'd just come in; she too had been out all night.

He didn't lose his temper. He lay there calmly, considering it. Weighing it the way a judge would, quite calm and objective, almost coldly. She hadn't been in long enough to lay back the covers. That was all there was to it. It was no reason for anger. She would explain where she had been and the why of it; she might lie about it, but she would explain. He would know if she were lying. He would have no difficulty in nailing the lie.

She'd been afraid of him when he came in last night. Because she had a guilty conscience? Not necessarily. He was still being calm about it. She had feared because she hadn't known it was he, his dragging steps were those of a stranger. It was fear of the unknown; not fear of him.

Her conscience hadn't been guilty. Because she'd demanded explanation of him, where had he been. She had a legitimate reason for her lateness; she'd come directly to him to explain. And he hadn't been there. Yet she'd forgiven him. She'd asked no further questions; she had taken him to comfort.

It was well after four when he stopped thinking, arose, and dressed. He hurried then, the shower and shave. He dressed in the suit he liked best; he didn't wear it often. It was distinctive, a British wool, gray with a faint overplaid of lighter gray, a touch of dim red. It fit him as well as had his dress uniforms; he'd had it made up for himself at Mel's tailors, when Mel first went to Rio, leaving his credit at its peak.

When he was dressed, he went into the living room. It was neat, everything in place; the sloven must have been here while he slept. The kitchen too was spotless. He decided to mix martinis; she liked them. This was a celebration night. They'd do it big; go out to dinner at some place swell, maybe Ciro's. He didn't have dinner clothes; he'd never bothered to have Mel's altered. He must see to that; he and Laurel were going to put on a campaign, although she didn't know it yet. He could help her as much as she could help him. A good-looking fellow who knew how to get what he wanted was what she needed. He'd get the spotlight for her and be satisfied to pick up the gold pieces that slid off the outer rim.

He mixed the cocktails, sampled one, and found its coldness good. Only one. He hadn't eaten, and he didn't want to spoil the evening by starting too soon. He brought in the evening paper from the doorstep, smiling to think how once the news had been more important to him than anything else. He smoked a cigarette, being careful to drop the ashes neatly into the tray, being careful to keep the chair in its place, the creases in his best suit. One cigarette and a careless reading of the paper; almost seven o'clock and she hadn't come, hadn't called.

She couldn't be going to stay away again. She wouldn't stay away without letting him know. For fifteen more minutes he riffled through the paper, reading with his eyes alone, wondering, anger beginning to take shape within his mind. Yet the words in his mind reiterated: she wouldn't, she couldn't.

Against his will, on stiff legs he stalked to the door, flung it open, and stepped out into the dim blue courtyard. He was afraid to look up to the balcony. The muscles of his eyes moved stiffly as his bones. He let out his breath in a slow, strangely relieved sigh. Her apartment was dark.

He returned to his, and he heard the phone ringing as he stepped into the hallway. He ran to answer, bumping against the doorway, wondering if it had been ringing long, fearing this too might be laid on him, missing her call.

He shouted his "Hello," and heard the answering "Hello," with irritation. A man's voice, Brub's voice. Brub saying a jumble of words, sorry to call so late, just got in, going to the club for dinner, could Dix make it?

He had no wish to make it. To sit in their goody-goody club through a wasted evening, with Sylvia staring at him and Brub trying to act as if he hadn't been made different by being chained to a woman. Even as Dix was making excuses, he heard the front door, and he revised his excuses quickly. He was a quick thinker, changing, "I'm afraid not, Brub," to "I'll tell you what, if I can I'll meet you there. You go on ahead. I have to find out what Laurel has up her sleeve." As if he too were chained. Quick thinking. If he could take Laurel to the club, as Brub's guests, he'd give her a big night and he wouldn't have to borrow the money from her to pay for it. Dix ended the conversation fast; his nerves jumping with the reasonless fear that she would leave before he could see her.

As he was hurrying to her, he wondered why she hadn't come to the bedroom. Wondering, his steps slowed, and he stopped in the doorway, a reasonless and terrifying fear chilling him. There might come a day when he would face strangers, quiet, businesslike strangers.

He called out, questioning, "Laurel?"

"Who were you expecting?"

It was Laurel, and he went in happily despite the quarrel underlying her voice. She was stretched out on the couch, her arms behind her head. She'd evidently just returned from whatever her afternoon business was; she was wearing a pin-checked sorrel suit; she'd unfastened the jacket; the narrow skirt was wrinkled above her long tapering legs. Her slant amber eyes were hostile on him. Her lip curled. "Going someplace?"

He didn't want to quarrel; he looked on her and was immediately filled with realization of his love for her. He loved her more than he had ever loved before. More than Brucie. For the first time he could think of Brucie while he thought of another woman. And he knew he loved this other woman.

"Sure," he smiled. But he didn't go to her. "How about a cocktail?" Get her in a good humor first; he didn't want to be pushed away. "I mixed martinis."

"Who with?"

For a moment he didn't get it. When he did, his smile was wide. She was jealous! She thought he had another woman. He wanted to laugh.

"With you, baby. Who else?" He did laugh then. "I'll get the mixings."

He felt so good, he whistled as he went to the icebox for the shaker. He caught up two glasses. She hadn't moved, and her eyes were no less hostile. "You haven't dressed up for me before," she said.

"We're going places tonight, baby," he told her. He poured carefully, the dry, dewy liquid. It even smelled good.

"Where? To a drive-in?"

His hand was steady. Only one drop spilled. She couldn't mean anything. She was trying to start a fight because she was jealous. Because he'd never taken her out and she thought he took other women out. He turned slowly, holding her glass.

"No drive-ins." Carefully he handed the glass to her. His eyes beheld her beauty, but he didn't touch her. "You aren't the drive-in type," he smiled down on her body.

She tasted the drink. "What type am I?" she asked sullenly. "The kind you wouldn't be caught dead with in a public place?"

He wouldn't quarrel. He'd keep his good nature. He went back to the chair with his drink. He smiled over the glass, "Definitely the bedroom type, beautiful. Haven't you enjoyed the honeymoon?"

"So it's over."

He had her where he'd wanted her all along. With him holding the reins. He'd been afraid before that she'd leave him; he'd been jumping through her hoops. It was good to be top man. "You weren't tired of it?"

She didn't answer; she demanded, "Where were you last night?"

He could have played it along, but he didn't. He didn't want to prolong her anger. "At Nicolai's," he said. Last night seemed years away. Brucie was dead, but it didn't matter any longer. Laurel was his love. "Drink up, baby. We've got to hurry. They're expecting us."

Deliberately she set her glass on the floor. "Who's expecting us?"

"Nicolais. We're to meet them at their beach club for dinner."

Her dark eyes were cold jewels. "So she's the one. That stiff-necked clotheshorse."

"Oh, Laurel!" he sighed. "What on earth are you getting at?"

She put down the words one after the other, like thuds on a drum. "You aren't the kind of man to stay out all night alone."

"Listen, Laurel." He was patient, even long-suffering. "Brub Nicolai was my best friend in the A.A.F. He's my best friend out here. His wife is his wife, and I'm no more interested in her than I am in the dame who sells me cigarettes at the drugstore or the old cow that manages these apartments, and right now I couldn't tell you what they look like. I went out to see the Nicolais last night only because you weren't here. They've asked us to have dinner with them tonight at their club. Now will you drink up that cocktail and get dressed so we can get to the club before it's too late?"

She picked up her glass and drained it slowly, set it back on the rug. "I'm not going," she said.

"But Laurel—" She ought to be beaten like a rug. "Why not?"

"Because I don't like stinking rich bastards and their stinking rich clubs."

"Laurel!" He was still patient; he clutched his patience. "They're not stinking rich bastards. They live in a little house, and their club is just a little informal club."

She snorted, "I know the Nicolais."

"Certainly, Laurel, the Nicolai family—"

"Rich society bastards."

"Will you listen to me?" He raised his voice. "Just because the family had money doesn't mean Brub has it. He doesn't. He just has his salary, his salary as a cop, that's all. God knows that can't be much. He and Sylvia don't have as much money as you have." He added quickly, "Or as I have."

"So now you've got money?" Her mouth was a sneer. "Did your check come in?"

"My check did come in," he said, holding his anger. "As a matter of fact, I got dressed thinking you'd be in early and we could celebrate tonight. Ciro's or any place you wanted. Then Brub called, and I thought you might prefer that. We can go to Ciro's anytime."

She yawned, insolently stretching her mouth wide. "I'm not going anyplace tonight," she said. "I'm going to eat something and go to bed. I'm tired."

He held in the words only for a moment. When he spoke they came out cold, quiet. "I guess you are. After your night out."

She hadn't known that he knew it. She turned her head. "What do you mean?"

"You didn't beat me home last night by very long, did you? Not even time to warm the bed."

Sullenness settled over her face like a hood. "It's none of your business," she said evenly.

He didn't speak. At that moment he couldn't trust himself to speak. He couldn't trust himself to look at her, at her insolent length, her stubborn mouth. It was his business. She was his woman; she belonged to him. He waited for her to say more, but only silence roiled about them. He knew better than to turn his eyes in her direction; when he did, he was walking towards her and he could feel the pain of his steeled fingers. There was no sound of his measured steps on the carpet. He was there standing over her before he knew. And his voice was one from far away, from out of the fog. "Laurel," it said. "Don't say that, Laurel."

Her smooth, cold eyes didn't waver. Yet something like a flicker of light or scrap of cloud went into them and out of them. So quickly you could not say it was there, because that quickly it was not there. Something that might have become fear. And he turned away his head. He had almost become angry; she was trying to make him angry, but he wouldn't let it happen. He was stronger than she. He stooped over and picked up her cocktail glass. His voice was closer in now. "How about another?"

"Might as well," she grudged.

He walked carefully to the table, poured the cocktail for her, carried it back to her.

"Thanks," she said. Not graciously. As sullen as before, the same sullen insolence in her eyes.

He smiled down at her. The bad moment was over, and he could smile. "How about it, baby? Think that one will put you back on your feet? It might be fun to drive out to the beach club—"

"It would stink." Deliberately she yawned. "If you can't be happy without your precious Nicolais, go on. I'm not going."

He drew a deep breath and forced a smile. She was acting like a two year old; you had to treat her like one. Ignore the tantrums. "Not without you. I'm taking you to dinner. If you feel that way, I'll phone Brub we can't make it." He started to the bedroom. "Shall I call Ciro's and reserve a table for"—he glanced at his watch—"ten o'clock?"

"Save your money," she yawned. "You can take me to a drive-in tonight." She was still yawning.

He stopped short. Slowly he turned to look at her. "I won't take you to a drive-in." He stated it flatly.

She flared, "Why not? What's the matter with a drive-in?"

"Nothing," he admitted readily. "But you're tired. You need a good dinner tonight. Not drive-in stuff."

"What's the matter with drive-in stuff? I eat at Simon's all the time, up on Wilshire."

It couldn't be deliberate. It was still part of the tantrum. He spoke slowly, carefully. "We're not going to eat there tonight."

She turned on the couch, lifted herself to one elbow. "What's the matter?" she demanded. "Are you afraid someone might see you there?"

She didn't mean a thing. She meant his big-shot friends, his rich friends like Mel. Someone might see him and think he was broke.

As if he had put the name in her mouth, she said, "You don't have to be afraid. Even Mel used to eat there when he was rocky."

He breathed easily. "I'm not rocky. I got a check today." She could get someone to cash it for him, or she could loan him enough for tonight. He built it. "Look, I get all dressed up to go places and do things. Come on, let's celebrate. We don't have to go to Ciro's. We'll go any place you say—the Kings, Tropics—"

She broke in again, "You look. I'm tired. I'm pooped. I don't want to get dressed up and go places. All I want is to go up to the drive-in—"

"We're not going up to the drive-in!" He didn't mean to shout. It came out in spite of himself. He closed his throat, and he kept his lips together in a tight line. His hands had begun to shake; quickly he thrust them into his coat pockets.

She was just looking at him out of her lozenge eyes, slyly looking at him, pleased that she'd made him lose his temper. "Okay," she said finally. "We'll go to the beach club."

He didn't believe what she'd said. His mouth fell open as if he were a character in a cartoon strip.

She said, "I changed my mind. We'll join the Nicolais." She got off the couch. She stretched like an animal, one of the big cats, a young golden puma. She came over to him there in the doorway. "Call and see if we're too late while I go change." She stood there beside him, but she didn't touch him. And he didn't touch her. There wasn't time. Not if they were to make it to the beach club. And he didn't want to go; unpredictably he had changed. Because she had? Because he wondered why she had. After she'd been so insistent about the drive-in.

He watched her walk away to the front door. She said, "Go on, call. I won't be long." And she went out.

He wanted to cry her back, to rush after her and bring her back here. They didn't have to go out. It was better for them to be alone, together. He had a feeling of desolation as she closed the door, as if she were gone forever. Although he knew she'd only run up to her own apartment to change, although he knew she would return, it was as if never again would she return to him.

He even took a step after her, but he reversed at once and went to the bedroom phone. He should have gone upstairs with her; he could have called from her phone. At least he should have tried to go with her. He'd never been in her apartment. He couldn't see what difference it would make; she came to his, but she insisted that the woman manager was a snoop. The old bag would throw them out if she thought anything went on between them. And the old bag's own apartment was at the right of the stairs; she knew everyone who went up and down those stairs, Laurel said. Mel's apartment was safer, isolated from prying eyes.

This wasn't the night to take issue with Laurel over any of her notions. He'd coddled her into a fairly decent humor, try to keep her there.

He looked up the beach club, dialed, waited while someone went to find Brub. He hoped it was too late, that the Nicolais had long ago gone home to bed. But it was only nine o'clock and Brub's voice denied his hope.

"What happened to you?" Brub asked.

"Laurel was delayed. Are we too late?" He hoped they were too late, but he couldn't deliberately try to call it off. Because he'd won the scrap with Laurel, he couldn't pull out of it now.

Brub said, "No. It's buffet tonight. We're serving until ten. Can you make it by then?"

"We'll be there right off."

"I'll try to hide out a couple of plates. Hurry up."

He hung up; they were committed now. He lit a cigarette and went back to the living room. There was still half a martini in the shaker. He drank it; it wasn't very good.

There was no reason to stand around here waiting. The old bag couldn't get her morals up if a man went to his girl's doorway to fetch her. Yet he didn't go. He started twice, but he didn't go. He didn't want another fight precipitated.

He was pushing out his second cigarette when she returned. He hadn't seen this dress before; it was some knit stuff, dull amber like her flesh, and it clung like flesh. It was cut low, sleeveless, and the short coat about her shoulders was cornflower blue. He whispered, "You're wonderful."

He went to her, but she sidestepped. "Later, Dix. There's no time to make up all over again. Let's go."

They were outside in the court before he remembered that his car was in the garage. "Do you want to wait here until I get it? Or shall we take yours?"

"I put mine up."

She went with him; he didn't want it, through the alley, the block to the far garage. But she was stubborn, and again there was the fear she would vanish if she weren't at his fingertips. She didn't say a word until they reached the garage, until he was opening the noiseless door. Then she said, "No one at the snoopery would ever hear what time you got home."

He laughed it off. "It's rather a jaunt."

She didn't go into the dark garage with him; she waited until he'd backed out before she got in the car. He headed to Wilshire. He said, "I'm surprised Mel would walk that far."

"He never put the car up. When's he coming back?"

"Who? Mel?"

"Yes."

"I don't know." He headed west on Wilshire. There was a faint haze in the night; the approaching headlights had a misty look. A few coming in from the beach showed golden fog lights.

"Don't you hear from him?"

"Good God, no." He laughed at the idea. "Can you imagine Mel writing me?"

"He might like to know how his apartment's getting along. And his car."

She was being deliberately nasty again. He said, "The rent I'm paying him, he should worry."

"You never gave me his address."

"I don't have it," he said. Why did she have to get on Mel? Why had he mentioned Mel tonight?

"You told me you'd give it to me."

"When I got it. He said he'd send it but he never has."

"Is that why you're holding his mail?"

She had snooped. His jaw was tight. He snapped, "That's why." She had snooped, so she knew what kind of mail was coming for Mel. He said, "Maybe he doesn't want his bills. Maybe that's why he doesn't send his address." He said, "I still don't know why you want his address."

"You don't know why," she slurred. Then her voice edged. "I'll tell you why. Because he went off owing me seven hundred dollars, that's why."

Dix was honestly amazed. "Mel owed you seven hundred dollars!"

"Yes. And I'd like to collect."

"Was Mel broke?" He couldn't believe it.

"He was always broke at the end of the quarter. Before his check came. This is the first time he didn't pay up as soon as it came."

They were in Santa Monica, and the haze was a little heavier. Not too much. The fronds of the palms in the parkway on the Palisades were dark against the mist-gray sky. The fog smelled of sea.

"Mel was a heel, but he paid his debts."

Again she could be meaning something, but her face, as the car rolled through the orange fog light on Ocean Avenue, meant nothing.

"It's probably the Rio mails," Dix dismissed it. He pushed the car right on the avenue and down the California Incline to the beach road. The car rolled down the dark, lonely Incline. No one walking there tonight. He said briskly, "I hope Brub saved us a lot of food. I'm hungry." He reached over and put his hand on her thigh. "I'm glad you decided to come, baby."

She hadn't thawed. She said, "I just came for the ride. But maybe I can entertain your best friend while you muse with his fancy wife."

He withdrew his hand. He said from his heart, "I don't want anyone but you, baby."

She was silent. Even her face said nothing.

# Chapter Five

## 1

THE club doors opened as if they had been seen approaching. They hadn't been. It was dark in the mist-hung forecourt, and they had been silent as they left the car. The opening of the door, too, was quiet, and some trick of silence held sound within the clubhouse for the moment before the girl appeared.

It was trick again that she appeared alone and within the veilings of mist assumed another's form and face.

He choked, "Brucie," yet beneath his breath the word was aloud.

He knew at once, even before speaking the word, that this was no apparition of Brucie. The word was no more than reflex. This was the little brown girl, the Banning girl, and she was not alone. Two young fellows followed her. They didn't notice Laurel and Dix standing in the mist and the night; the trio cut across to a car on the opposite side of the court, laughing together.

He knew that Laurel had heard the name even before she spoke. "Who's Brucie?"

"A girl—I used to know." He walked away quickly from the words and the memory. Into the lighted club, the clear, unmisted light of the living. He didn't know or care that Laurel followed him. Yet he was grateful to find her there. He was all right again in the light. He smiled at her. "Come on, let's find Brub fast. I'm starving."

Brub lifted a greeting hand from a table by the far windows of the dining room. Dix took Laurel's arm. "There they are." Laurel hadn't softened any; there was a sulkiness in the arm he touched. She'd get over the mood; put some food into her and she'd cheer up. She hadn't come along just to stage a scene; that hadn't been the purpose of her reversal of mood. Yet he looked at her with a touch of apprehension as they reached the table. He was reassured; Laurel was civilized. She had on the same company-polite smile that Sylvia was wearing.

She didn't revert until after dinner and leisurely coffee. Until he asked her to dance. Even then he was the only one could know. "You've forgotten your manners, Dix," she said, so sweetly, so ladylike. "A guest dances first with his hostess."

It was mild enough, and he played up. "If Sylvia will do me the honor."

"He's a wonderful dancer," Laurel cooed.

She didn't know; she'd never danced with him. But as long as she didn't act up any more than this, he was satisfied.

Sylvia's long and lovely lines fit well against him, just as he'd known they would the first time he saw her. He was stirred by the touch of her, almost exulted by it. If she were not Brub's wife, if he were to be alone with her—the fact that she consciously withheld herself from intimacy was knowledge that she too was aware of body. They danced well and easily, whatever awareness lay beneath the mind and perceptions.

He knew the absurdity of his reaction; he had a woman, a far richer woman than this. He had no need of Sylvia, and yet there was need, the sensual need of pitting his mind against the mind of another. Until this moment he had not realized his itch for the chase. Deprivation had made him jumpy these last days. Even in this incident which could not be furthered, he had begun to soar. He was breathing as a man could breathe when he was lifted into the vastness of sky, when he knew himself to be a unit of power, complete in himself, powerful in himself.

Sylvia said, "Laurel is very lovely, Dix."

Her commonplace words brought him thudding to earth. Brought him to annoying consciousness of the noisy room, the disturbing shuffle of dancers' feet, the coils and scraps of conversation, the metallic music of the phonograph. He said, "Yes," although for the moment he hardly knew to what he was assenting. His inner ear echoed her statement and he said with more enthusiasm, "Yes, isn't she? Something special." He turned Sylvia in order that he too might look upon Laurel. He had not ever seen her in dance motion. She should be something special.

She was not dancing. She was sitting with Brub at the table, their heads together, their words intent. He didn't understand. He knew that Brub had risen to dance with Laurel as Sylvia and Dix left the table. But they hadn't danced; they had remained together to talk; they were talking as if they had waited a long time for this moment. "You've known Laurel before!" he said quickly. He didn't mean it to sound suspicious, but he spoke too quickly.

Sylvia's answer was unperturbed. "We've met her. When she was married to Henry St. Andrews. I didn't realize it when you introduced me at your apartment. Not until she mentioned Gorgon. We met her at Gorgon's."

"Who is Gorgon?"

"He's a lawyer." She wasn't as easy now, she was making up words. "A friend of Henry St. Andrews. And Raoul Nicolai, Brub's oldest brother. We don't know them well. We don't travel in that crowd. Can't afford it."

He remembered it now. Gorgon had had opinions on the case. Laurel had quoted Gorgon's opinions. And he remembered he'd seen the name. It must be the same name. Thomas Gorgonzola. Criminal lawyer. A name to conjure with in L.A. courts, a name that meant a feature to the newspapers. He smiled; not Sylvia, not anyone would know the meaning of that smile. Laurel's friend, the great criminal lawyer.

"What is St. Andrews like?" he asked curiously.

"I didn't like him," Sylvia answered. She wasn't hesitant any longer; she was on even keel. "One of those spoiled young men, too much money, mamma's darling, an ego inflated by too much attention and absolutely no discipline all of his life."

"Heavy drinker?" St. Andrews sounded like Mel. Laurel hated the first; it was a cinch she hadn't had any doings with Mel.

"That goes without saying. Liquor is such a nice substitute for facing adult life. I understand Laurel took quite a beating."

"Yes," he agreed. "She doesn't say much, but I gathered that."

"She wasn't good enough for the sacrosanct St. Andrews. And anyone with a functioning mind is an insult to their irrationality. You know, before I met Brub, I was afraid he'd be that kind. The Nicolais and the St. Andrews—all that clan."

"Aren't you?" He was a little surprised.

She laughed. "What you said! My grandfather was delivering babies, and not getting paid for it, while the clans were grabbing everything that might turn into silver dollars. No, I'm just a poor girl, Dix. And fortunately Brub's a throw-back to when the Nicolais worked for a living."

The music ended. He would have liked to continue the talk, to ask more about Gorgon. But she started to the table, and he followed. The dark head of Brub and the glowing head of Laurel separated as they approached. He put Sylvia in her chair. "Thank you," he said with mock formality. "It was indeed a pleasure." He sat down beside her. "Now that my manners have been made, let me tell you it really was a pleasure." There was a drink in front of him, and he sampled it. "What's the matter, Brub? Laurel step on your new shoes?"

Laurel said, "I was tired. I didn't want to dance." She hadn't lost her hostility, although her words seemed simple statement of fact. Her eyes were watching him with the same intensity as earlier. He ignored it. He said pleasantly, "I'm sorry. I wanted to dance with you. Couldn't you take one little spin?"

"I'm too tired," she said. She wasn't sorry. She had no intention of dancing with him, of giving in to him.

It didn't matter. He could handle her later. He could handle anyone. He was Dix Steele. There was power in him.

"Who is Brucie?"

He was shocked that she would ask, that she would deliberately instigate a quarrel before Brub and Sylvia. He'd even forgotten the episode in the doorway; she too should have forgotten it until later tonight when they were alone, when he could explain it in private. His eyes went quickly to her, but she wasn't asking the question of him, and he realized she'd tricked it in a small, curious voice, asked it to all.

Brub could have answered her, Sylvia could have, but both were silent. Brub was looking into his drink, turning it in his worried hand. Sylvia was shocked as Dix, her eyes were wide on him. It was up to him to answer. He said it quietly, "She was a girl I knew a long time ago. That Brub and I knew. In England." He was furious, but he was quiet. He'd told her that much outside. She shouldn't have nuzzled the name, kept it alive in her consciousness. He completed her knowledge. "She's dead."

He opened his eyes on her as he spoke, and he saw the shock come into hers. He wanted to shock her. He wouldn't have said it otherwise, not bluntly, not out like that. He didn't know if there were fear in her as well as shock; you couldn't tell; it was hard to tell what lay behind gem-smooth, gem-hard, amber eyes.

"Dead," she repeated, as if she didn't believe him. "But she was—"

He smiled, "That girl wasn't Brucie." He explained to Sylvia, to Brub who had looked up at him again. "As we were coming in tonight, we saw that girl, the one who was here that other evening. You knew her name, Sylvia, and she reminded you of Brucie, remember, Brub?"

Sylvia said, "The Banning girl."

"Yes." His voice wasn't quite steady remembering that moment in the mystery of the night and fog. "She looked so much like Brucie tonight, it—" He smiled ruefully. "It was rather startling."

He was pleased now that Laurel had brought up the name when she did. Brub and Sylvia were corroboration of the fact that there was no Brucie in his life; Laurel might have doubted him if he'd explained it away in private. He was pleased too that the name had remained with her, that it had given her jealousy. He was still important to her. She had thought he was shaken because he'd run into a girl out of his past.

Again he asked her to dance, and this time she didn't refuse. He held her closely, he said to her hair, "You didn't think there was anyone else for me, did you, baby?"

"I don't know what I thought," she said. "How does anyone ever know what they really think?" She was defensive, but she was weary; it was in the strands of her voice.

He said, "Let's go home."

"All right," she agreed.

He didn't wait for the music to end; he danced her to the table and saw Sylvia and Brub move apart, in the same fashion that Laurel and Brub had earlier. He didn't wonder at the repetition; only briefly did it occur to him that Brub must be in one of his confidential moods. And that Brub too must be tired tonight, otherwise he'd be cutting capers on the dance floor.

## 2

IT DIDN'T occur to Dix to wonder why Brub was tired. Not until he and Laurel had ridden in the silence of her weariness almost to the apartment. He'd been thinking of Laurel, watching her as she rested there in the corner of the seat, her eyes closed, her lips parted as if she slept. He'd been thinking of her beauty and her fire, and tonight, her lack of fire. Thinking without thoughts, conscious of her and of the fact that this many mist-dulled streets must be covered before he could put the car at the curb, until he and Laurel could be alone.

He didn't consciously bring Brub to memory. It was one of those minnows of thought, darting through the unruffled pond of his thinking. But why should Brub be beaten? The case was closed, insofar as work activity was concerned. In the files of unfinished business there was an entry; girl murdered, murderer unknown. There were plenty of like entries, another wouldn't mean that a young fellow playing cop should have all the high spirits knocked out of him. Plenty of reasons why Brub could have been tired, he could have thrown one the night before, he could have sat up reading all night; he and Sylvia could have continued their dissension, if there had been one, far into the dawn. Or they could have pitied Dix far into the dawn. Because of Brucie.

And that had been only last night, the revelation of Brucie's death. Dix should have been the one holding his head in his hands. But he knew how to get away from trouble, from grief and from fear. He knew better than to indwell with it. He was smart.

He said aloud, "I don't know why everyone should be so tuckered tonight. I'm not."

She wasn't asleep. She didn't open her eyes, but she said, "Why should you be? You slept all day."

It wasn't much further home. And he waited to answer, waited until they could be alone. It wasn't worth while to whittle off little edges of disagreement; you must get at the roots. As soon as he found out what was in back of her hostility, he would uproot it. They'd have it out tonight, before she slept.

He said, "We're here."

He held the door, and she slid under the wheel to get out of the car. She might have slept on the way home, her eyes were half-closed yet. She walked ahead of him under the arch into the blue-lighted patio, dulled in tonight's mist. She must have been half-asleep for she didn't turn to Mel's apartment. She was starting back to the steps when he caught her arm, asking softly, "Where you going, baby?" He turned her, holding her arm, "You're walking in your sleep."

She stood there quietly while he opened the door, but she waited to enter, waited until he touched her again and explained, "We're home, honey. Wake up."

He had left the lamp burning in the living room. He shut out the blue mist and turned to the welcome of the light. It was good to be home. With her. "Go get undressed and I'll fix you a drink."

"I don't want a drink," she said. A little shiver twisted her shoulders.

"Something hot," he said. "Milk? Coffee?"

"Coffee," she said. "I'd like coffee. Hot, black coffee."

"Coming up!" He filled the electric percolator in the kitchen. He'd make it in the bedroom. With her. He fixed the tray and hurried back to her.

She hadn't started to undress. She was sitting on the edge of the bed, just sitting there looking into the monotone of the rug.

He plugged in the percolator. "Be ready in a minute. Why don't you get undressed while it's perking? I'll serve you in bed, solid comfort."

She didn't make any move, not even to take off her coat. She just looked up at him. Not saying anything, not even with her eyes. Not even hostility now in her eyes.

He came over to her, and he sat down beside her on the bed. "Look," he said gently. "Get it off your chest. What's bothering you?"

She shook her head, and her hair fell across her cheek. As if mist were bright as sun, it obscured her face.

"It isn't fair not to tell me, Laurel," he continued. "You don't give me a chance. How can I explain if you don't let me know what's the trouble?"

Her sigh was audible. She started to say, "What's the good—" but he stopped her, turning her to face him.

"You're the most important thing in the world to me, Laurel. No matter what it is, I want to get it right with you." He didn't mean to say much, he meant to keep it light, but he couldn't when he had touched her, when he was looking into her face. "I couldn't bear to lose you, Laurel. I couldn't take it."

She studied his face while she released her shoulders gently from his hands. She could see in him truth of what he had said. Her voice was very tired. "All right, Dix," she said. "Let's talk about it. Let's start at the beginning. Where were you last night?"

That was easy. "But I told you. At Nicolai's."

"Where were you after you left Nicolai's?"

She'd been checking up on him. He got up from the bed and began to walk the room. She was Laurel, but she was a woman and she was snooping on him. His laugh was short. "So you didn't believe me. You checked with Brub. That's what you two were talking about."

"That was part of it," she admitted.

"What did Brub tell you?"

"You needn't get annoyed. I didn't ask him outright. I simply found out you'd been there early and left early."

"You didn't believe me," he accused.

147

"I didn't believe you'd come from Nicolai's at four in the morning in the shape you were in," she said flatly.

The coffee was beginning to bubble. It was a small sound, a bubble forming, breaking, a small, annoying sound. He shut it out of his ears. He wouldn't let it start roaring. He didn't have to listen to sounds any longer; he had Laurel. He had her voice and her presence to shut away sound. He could explain to her, and he didn't mind explaining. He didn't mind anything that would keep Laurel near to him.

"How much did Brub tell you?" he asked. "Did he tell you the news he gave me last night?" If Brub had, she wouldn't be asking these questions. She'd be avoiding the subject as did Brub and Sylvia. He was pleased that Brub had kept silent; it was better that he tell Laurel himself; it was another tie to her. "No, I didn't come right home from Nicolai's. I couldn't. You see, Brub had just told me that Brucie was dead."

Her eyes widened. With a kind of terror of disbelief.

"I couldn't see anyone. I was too shocked. I drove. Just drove. I don't know where, up the beach, I guess. I remember hearing the water." The shush of the water, the hush of a girl's voice. His own voice was uneven. "That's why I came home—the way I did."

She said, "No." In disbelief. In pity. And then she said, "Brucie must have meant a lot to you."

"She did."

"More than anyone."

He came to her swiftly, knelt before her, taking her hands. "That was true until I met you, Laurel. But there's never been anyone like you. Not ever." His hands tightened over hers. "Marry me, Laurel. Will you? We're meant for each other. You know it. You knew it the first time we looked at each other, just the way I knew it. Will you, Laurel?"

She had released her hands. And the weariness on her face

wasn't because she was tired; it was because she was sad. She shook her head. "It's no good, Dix. If I married you, I wouldn't have a dime."

"But I—" He didn't get a chance to build a dream.

She looked at him out of seeing eyes. "You don't have a dime either, Dix. Don't bother to lie. I know you. Yes, I knew you the first time I looked at you, just like you knew me. Because we're just alike. We're out to get it, and we don't care how we get it."

He had left her. He was walking around again, listening to what she had to say, hating what she knew, hating that there wasn't truth with which to demolish it. Because he couldn't lie to her now. She knew too much.

"I thought I could get it marrying St. Andrews. All the money in the world and a position where I could look down my nose at the small-town big shots that looked down their noses at me when I was a kid. I didn't know how hard it was. I couldn't take it. The St. Andrews weren't a bit different from the Buckmeisters back in Nebraska. They just had more money and bigger noses. So I got out. But I'm still going after what I want. And I'll get it. I'll get it on their money, and don't think that doesn't burn them. And when I get there, I'll be up so high I won't even know they're down there under my nose." There was an excitement in her as well as hate. She was getting there. That was all the business she'd been attending to while he slept; she knew she was getting there. When she did, she'd carry him along. But he couldn't risk waiting; when she did, there might be someone else. He walked around trying to figure what he could do. If he had Uncle Fergus's money, he could have her right now. They'd go to the top together. If there were some way to get the money that was his, that was going to be his. He heard her voice again.

"—I don't know how you got rid of Mel so you could take over here. I don't even care. But I know you're living on borrowed time. I know Mel will come back from wherever he is—"

"He's in Rio."

"Rio or taking the cure again, I don't know."

"He's in Rio," he insisted.

"Maybe he finally went. He'd been talking Rio ever since I met him three years ago, and before that. The big job he was going to take over in Rio. Next week. Next month. Maybe you got him to take it, I don't know. Anyway, you fell into the apartment and the clothes he didn't want and his car. How you wangled it, I don't know; he wouldn't give his best friend the cork out of a bottle. But he's going to come back and take them all again, and then what are you going to do? Move in on somebody else? You can't carry a wife with you living that way. Get a job? You don't want a job. And you couldn't get one that would pay enough to keep me in war paint. I'm expensive, Dix."

He was choked up. "My uncle—"

"What uncle?"

"My uncle, back in Princeton. You're wrong about that. I've got an uncle, and he's got the chips."

"You haven't got them," she said cruelly. "Don't try to tell me he's cutting you in. I know guys in the chips. They don't keep a girl cooped up in an apartment. They're out spending."

In the silence, the roar of the coffee percolator blurred his ears. He saw her as she walked over to the table. He was grateful when she shut out the sound. She drew two cups, handed one to him.

"Let's face it, Dix. It's been swell but—"

Panic made his voice too loud. "You're not calling quits?"

She spoke quickly, stammering a little. "No, no. I didn't mean that. But it can't be for keeps, Dix. You know that as well as I. I'm not saying that if you had half the money that stinker of an ex had, I wouldn't marry you. Want to marry you." She finished her coffee and drew another cup.

Automatically he said, "Don't drink too much of that. You won't be able to sleep."

"I don't expect to sleep very well." There was sadness in her voice again.

She moved to the dressing-table bench as he went to the end table. He put sugar and cream in his coffee. He stirred it. The spoon whorled the liquid, churned it as a storm churned the sea. He put away the spoon, and he drank some of the coffee. He said, "You're not telling me everything, Laurel. You're keeping something back. You're through with me."

"No, no, I'm not," she protested quickly. He ought to tell her to stop saying that—*no, no, no.*

She went on haltingly, "There's only one thing. If I land what I'm after, it'll mean leaving town."

He waited until he could speak quietly. "What kind of a job is it?"

"It's a show. Musical. They're casting it here on the coast. I've got a good chance." Life returned to her eyes. "It means Broadway—after that, the pictures. Starring, not a peasant in the background."

"Broadway." He could go back East. He could get things fixed up with Uncle Fergus! Everything was going to be all right. He was sick of California anyhow. "Broadway," he repeated and he smiled. "Baby, that's wonderful. Wonderful."

A childish surprise came into her face at his reaction. He finished his coffee, set down the cup. He walked with excitement. "That's terrific, Laurel. Why didn't you tell me? I've got to go back home in a couple of months anyway. You're right about my uncle. The old skinflint has hardly given me enough to eat on; that's why I've been pinching the pennies. And if it weren't for Mel letting me use this place, I'd have been in a furnished room somewhere. I'd never have had a chance to lay eyes on you. Good old Mel."

He was burned up with the radiant promise of the future. Even if he couldn't fix things with Uncle Fergus, by that time she'd have so much money she wouldn't need the St. Andrews' income, she wouldn't need Dix's income. She'd move him in, and he'd get a chance to pick off the outer leaves of dough. The rightness of it all laid a sanctity on it. And he could embellish a bit now, because of the rightness it would ring true. "We'll be hitting the east coast about the same time. You're wrong about my not wanting a job, I'm used to working. I was raised on work." He laughed. "You don't know my Uncle Fergus! The only reason I've been laying off a year was to get a chance at writing a book. Now I'll go back and take on the job he wants to give me, and it'll pay for more than your war paint. He's got a factory that turns out stocks and bonds. He wants me to handle the advertising. That means New York, baby," he grinned, "and I think by the time your run is over with, we'll be doing some California advertising. I'll be around, Laurel!" She laid down her cup just in time. He caught her tightly in his arms. "Laurel," he was laughing. He was half-crying. "Laurel, I knew we were meant to be. Forever. For always."

She didn't say anything. She couldn't say anything. She was trembling within the cup of his arms.

# 3

His sleep was restless. Even with her beside him, dreams drove him fretfully to the surface of the night. Too often. She too was restless. For he heard her stirring each time he half-awakened, heard her breath of wakefulness, not sleep. The dreams were shapes in the mist. He could not remember them when he awoke at last from the final stretch of deep if uneasy sleep.

He hadn't slept long enough. She was gone, as she was always gone when he awoke these days. There was no sun in which to remember her. The morning was a dirty gray rag. He felt cramped within the misshapen room. The dregged coffee cups were there, one on the dressing table, one by the tray.

He had to get out of here. He showered, hating the sound of the rushing water; shaved, hating the buzz of the razor. He dressed quickly, not caring what he put on. He had no plan, only to get out of this room, to get away from the unremembered shape of his dreams.

He didn't take the car. In order to breathe, in order to put motion into the staleness of his body. He didn't know why he should feel this way; everything had been right, everything was going to be right. Laurel had made it right. There'd be a few weeks of separation while she was on the road, but that was unimportant. A separation would whet the emotions of both. Absence was a heady spice.

He felt better by the time he'd walked as far as Wilshire, and he continued up Beverly Drive to his favorite delicatessen. He turned in there. He was suddenly hungry. He was a little ahead of the noon crowd. He ordered salami and swiss on rye and a lot of coffee. It was when he was paying for it, breaking his last ten, that he realized he must do something about the torn check. The envelope was in his pocket. He had automatically transferred it with the rest of his stuff when he dressed.

He was pretty sure he'd need help to cash it. He'd only been in the bank twice in Beverly; no one knew him well enough to accept a mutilated check. The deal called for Brub's help, a Nicolai and a cop ought to throw a little weight.

He finished eating, left the delicatessen, and went into the nearest drugstore. He called Santa Monica first, but there was no answer. It was a guess, but he called the Beverly Hills station. It wasn't Brub's bailiwick but at least they could steer him to the right number.

The cop who answered said Detective Nicolai wasn't there. Dix hadn't expected Brub to be there. He said, "I know. I just want to find out what number to call to get in touch with him." He thought the cop was stupid but the cop was thinking the same thing of him; it finally cleared up: Brub was in Beverly but he'd gone out to lunch. The cop didn't know where.

Dix was irritated when he left the booth. It shouldn't have taken that long to find out that Brub was in the neighborhood. He didn't want to go sit in the police station to wait; he wasn't in the mood for that kind of amusement today. He hadn't anything to do. He could probably run into Brub if he made the rounds of the nearby eating spots. It would be better to run into him instead of seeking him out. Make it casual.

He was lucky. He found Brub in the second place, the one he called the Ice House. Always a carved cake of ice in the window. Dix said surprised, "Well, look who's here!" Before he saw the other man, the lean-visaged Lochner. Before he wondered why the two were together again in Beverly Hills.

Brub was surprised to see Dix. "Where'd you come from?"

"A guy gets hungry." He spoke to Lochner, "How d'you do, Captain Lochner."

Brub moved over in the booth, and Dix sat by him. It was invitation to join them. He had to eat again, but he didn't care. He ordered a chicken sandwich and a bottle of beer. It was a good omen, running into Brub as he'd wanted, not having to seek him out. It made him feel more cheerful. "More trouble in Beverly?" he asked.

"No," Brub shook his head, took a big bite of spaghetti, blurring his words. "Same old case."

"You're still working on that?" He was surprised.

"We don't give up," Lochner said in his flat voice.

He really was surprised. "It's still important enough that the head of Homicide is giving special attention to it?"

Lochner said, "We aren't going to let it happen again."

"Then you honestly believe it stems from this neighborhood."

154

Lochner shrugged. "It's the last clue we have."

"Seems rather hopeless," Dix said kindly.

Brub's words were audible again. "We pick up a little every time we check."

Dix didn't show any disturbance. He was as calm as an innocent bystander. "But where do you check? How?"

"We've been talking to the help again. At the drive-in where he stopped with her that night."

He was more calm. When there was anything to face, he could play up to it. "Any luck?"

There wasn't. He could tell by Brub's expression. Lochner said, "There may be. Nicolai's got a good idea there." The chief left it for Brub to tell.

Brub said, "I don't know that it will amount to anything. But in these neighborhood spots, a lot of the same faces recur pretty regularly. Down at Doc Law's, for instance, in the canyon, you get to know people just seeing them over and again. I got to thinking about it. There must have been some of the regulars around that night when he took Mildred in for coffee." He let out a gust of breath. "God, the nerve of him! Walking in there, facing all those lights, and gambling no one would remember what he looked like."

"Like you and me," Dix dared, "an ordinary man."

Brub nodded slowly. "Yeah. An ordinary man. With the nerve of a jet pilot." He took another bite of spaghetti fast and talked through it. "My idea, whatever good it is, is to have the help ask questions of the regulars when they come in. Were they at the drive-in the night of the murder, and did they notice the couple?"

"Not bad," Dix said, as if he were thinking about it. "And I suppose you're hoping this fellow is a repeater too."

"Yeah. That would be a break." Brub was exasperated quickly. "What a break, but no chance. Except for his nerve."

"You mean he might have the nerve to walk in again."

"Yeah."

"And you think the help would spot him in that case."

"I'm sure they would. At least I think they would. They're keyed up to remember. The little girl—Gene, her name is—is sure she'd know him if he came in again. She says she'd know him if she ever saw him. Only she can't describe him."

"The trouble with people in these cases," Lochner droned, "is that they're not articulate."

"What about the tailor?" Dix asked.

"What tailor?" Brub frowned.

"The one you told me about. The one that saw this fellow and that earlier girl come out of the movie in Hollywood." He'd nearly said the Paramount. He took a swallow of his beer. "Are you working on him too?"

Brub shook his head. "He wasn't close enough to them to be any good at identification. The guy could go in and be measured for a suit and he wouldn't know."

"He might," Dix smiled. "Mightn't he? A tailor might be expected to recognize the shoulders or the body length, don't you think?"

Lochner hmmed, and Brub thought that the tailor might. Dix had given them an idea. And welcome to it. Brub was thinking out loud again, "Walking right into that battery of lights. What a nerve!"

Dix said, "Maybe he didn't intend to do anything to her. Maybe it wasn't so much nerve but no intention."

"We've considered that," Brub said thoughtfully. "But it doesn't fit the pattern. He picked them up to kill them. It wasn't ever without intention."

"According to your reconstruction."

Brub's smile was a little abashed. "I don't think I'm far off base. He's first of all a killer, that we know. He kills because he's a killer." He tallied on. "He's a gambler. He's reckless. I mean he'll take chances, like that drive-in, or taking the other girl to the movies. But he's not so reckless that he doesn't realize his chances; it's the recklessness we had at the sticks during the war. We took chances, but we were sure, God willing, that we'd pull out of them."

"He's an ex-serviceman," Lochner supplied.

Dix raised his eyebrows. When Lochner didn't explain, he said, "That's something new."

"Ten to one," Lochner said. "He's the right age, good healthy specimen, average. The average were in the service."

"He's a nice-looking fellow, nice clothes," Brub said. "We know that from our inarticulate observers. He's well off, he has a car. He has a pleasant approach. We know that too, or these girls wouldn't have let him pick them up. Except maybe that first one."

"What was a fellow like you reconstruct doing on Skid Row?"

"That's one of the things we don't know," Brub admitted.

"Maybe he was slumming," Lochner said.

"Maybe he knew he was off on a kill," Brub was feeling it out. "Maybe he didn't want to do it. Maybe he thought it wouldn't matter so much if he picked a girl that didn't matter."

"And after the first time, he didn't care?" Dix asked soberly.

"It wasn't the first time," Lochner said with authority.

Dix's eyes slewed to him, letting his surprise show through.

"It was too professional," Lochner explained. He picked up his check. "I'm going back to the station and go over those Bruce reports again. Coming?"

Bruce reports. Bruce wasn't an uncommon name. There must be a hundred thousand Bruces in the United States. Hundreds in L.A. Dix didn't show any reaction to the name. He went right on eating the sandwich. They could have been examining him, putting out this information to get reaction from him. There was no reason for them to have any suspicion of him. There was nothing at all that made him open to suspicion. Absolutely nothing.

"I'll be along shortly," Brub said. "Soon as I finish eating." He'd ordered apple pie and coffee. The girl was bringing them now.

Dix waited until Lochner was at the door. "Smart guy," he said. "The best." Brub was testing the pie.

Dix got away from the subject, onto a natural one. "You and Laurel hit it up pretty chummy last night, didn't you?"

Brub didn't grin it off. He said seriously, "I like her."

"I didn't realize you and Sylvia had known her before."

"Just met. Never had a chance to talk to her until last night."

"You did pretty well last night. Looked like a serious confab." He was fishing. But he could fish openly; Laurel was his girl. He didn't catch anything.

Brub said, "I have my serious moments."

Dix said, "Won't do you any good. Looks like Laurel and I aren't going to be around much longer."

Brub wiped his mouth. His eyes were opened in surprise.

"Didn't she tell you about the show she's going into? And it's about time for me to head back to New York."

"You're going back East?" Brub was surprised. He added with mock rue, "Just when I thought we had you sold on California." He took another bite. "What's the trouble? Mel Terriss coming home?"

Laurel had talked to Brub about Mel Terriss. Brub wouldn't have had the name so glibly if she hadn't. Harping on Mel. Wondering aloud to Brub if Mel was in Rio? He bit his anger between his teeth. "I haven't heard from Mel. No telling about him. I've got to go back and get refinanced." He remembered the check. "By the way, Brub, wonder if you could help me out?" He was quick. "This isn't a touch, pal. I tore up my check, got the envelope mixed in with a bunch of ads. I'm too stony to wait for Uncle Fergus to send another, and the old boy wouldn't wire money if I were selling pencils. Would you want to vouch for me at the bank here?"

"Sure. I don't know the rules, but it's worth a try." Brub picked up both tabs. Dix took them out of his hand. "I'm not that stony. My turn."

The gray day settled over them as they emerged. It was depressing; no matter how good you'd been feeling, to step into this dirty wash was depressing.

The bank was only across the street. He'd borrowed trouble about the check. There was none. Brub's identity was good. The bank manager was pleasant, saying, "I don't know why anyone should be penalized for making a mistake. As long as you have all the parts." You could tell by his manner he considered Dix an honest young fellow, a friend of the Nicolais was certain to be all of that.

He felt better with the two-fifty in his billfold. The day even looked brighter. He said, "Thanks, Brub. Thanks a million." He was ready to go. He'd buy a present for Laurel. He'd never given her anything. He couldn't splurge, not on these peanuts, but he could buy her something, if only one orchid. He'd drape her in orchids someday.

It was Brub who was making the delay. Brub who blurted it out, "Those reports."

He knew what was coming. He felt the gray close in on him again, but he showed only polite courtesy.

"Would you want to look them over? They're the reports on Brucie." Brub was rattling. He was embarrassed. Expecting Dix to break down? Or ashamed that he was suspecting a friend, a friend he had no reason to suspect? A shocked, grave look was the right one from Dix.

"I was talking to Lochner about her. I couldn't help talking about her, I was knocked off my pins when I heard the news. He cabled for a report on the case from the London police." Brub was speaking more slowly now. Because Dix hadn't burst into sobs? Because he was warning Dix? "He thought it might help us out. That maybe Brucie was one of a series, like our series. It's far-fetched, but the killer might have been an American. England was full of G.I.'s at that time. Maybe even a California man."

He asked only one question, "Was she one of a series?"

Brub's face was torn. "They don't know. There was a series but it didn't start right after Brucie. A couple of months—and then it began. The same pattern. A strangler."

"He was never caught?"

"No, he was never caught." Brub hesitated. "After six months it stopped. As suddenly as it had begun. Maybe he was shipped back home."

"And did it start then, over on this side?" It was a good question. Brub slurred it. "N-no."

No series, no pattern. Isolated cases. They hadn't caught up with the isolated cases. On the east coast. Or had they? Was Brub keeping quiet because it might sound too pointed? Why should Brub suspect him?

He knew he'd better get away. He was beginning to grow angry. Brub had no business suspecting him. Yet he didn't believe that was any part of it. Only a part of his own depression. He said, "I don't think I could take the reports, Brub. You understand?"

"Yes, Dix." Brub's face showed sympathy. "See you soon."

He watched Brub's stocky figure roll away in the crowd. He shook his head, regretfully. Poor guy. Going around in circles trying to find an invisible man. Brub must be desperate if he were suspecting his best friend. Dix felt better. He rambled down Beverly Drive, shopping the windows as if he were one of the chattering females obstructing the walks. At Leonard's he took a chance, turned in. The moment he'd decided to chance it, he felt right. The whole trouble with these past weeks was playing it safe; that was what love did to you, love and being stony; and the result, the megrims.

He walked in, and he put it over smooth. Too bad he couldn't get a suit out of it, but he did well enough. Several jackets, navy flannel, white tweed, gabardine in tan, pinks was what it was called a couple of years ago; shirts, ties, a nice haul all wrapped up to be shipped to Rio. Dix Steele signing for it, he'd established that fact when he first moved into Mel's. Dix Steele taking care of Mel's affairs while Mel was in Rio. Maybe the credit was strained a bit but he brushed that off, first of the month, check coming any day now. And Mel wanting some of Leonard's good stuff, Rio togs didn't suit him. A dust of flattery and man-to-man and gab, and he'd mail the box himself as he was on his way to the post office. His car just around the corner.

He wished for the car as he lugged the heavy box down the street. He'd get the address label ripped off as soon as he got home, before Laurel snooped around and saw it. She might try writing Mel at Avenida de Perez, nice-sounding street. Letters could go astray. However, she might be anxious enough to cable. Not so good. Besides he'd said he hadn't known Mel's address.

He shifted the box. He should have had it delivered. But he wanted the navy flannel jacket for tonight, wanted to show her that the check was bigger than she thought it was. He shifted it again as he passed the Beverly Theatre. And he stopped. It was only four o'clock. Laurel didn't ever return until six, nearer seven. There was a special showing of some big picture, hence there was continuous run. He hadn't seen a picture in weeks. He went in.

It was after six when he came out. The street lamps were lighted in the early, hazy dark. He was a damn fool for walking, not bringing the car. There was no crosstown bus line that serviced his neighborhood. He had to walk it, carrying the awkward box. No taxis in sight.

It wasn't far, but his arms ached when he reached the dark apartment. Automatically he looked to the balcony. Her apartment too was dark. He went in and lighted his. He wondered if she'd tried to call, to tell him she'd be late. Not tonight. After the wrangle of last night, she'd get home tonight. She'd go places with him. He took another shower, leaving the door open to listen for the phone.

He dressed elegantly, the gray flannels, the navy coat. He looked like a million dollars. And felt like it. Although it was past seven and she still hadn't phoned. He was certain that she was coming, otherwise he'd have heard from her before now.

He went out and mixed himself a tall, comfortable highball. He stretched comfortably in the chair, took up the evening paper. Tonight he wasn't going to get annoyed waiting for her, he felt good.

She didn't come at all.

# 4

Discomfort wakened him. He'd fallen asleep in the chair. His legs were cramped; his neck was rigid. He turned off the lamp, and the windows became gray. He didn't care what time it was. He didn't think about time. There was no reason to go again into the court, to gaze up at her apartment. He wouldn't know if she were there or not. She hadn't been there at four. Her lights wouldn't be on now if she had slunk back like the alley cat she was.

She could wait. He was too foggy now to knock her awake and demand explanation. Even if foggy, he was smart. No one in the Virginibus Arms was going to remember him at Laurel Gray's door.

He flung himself fully dressed on the bed. If he could sleep without taking anything, he would. He didn't want to be put out. He must be alerted for the ringing of the telephone.

His sleep was sodden, although much too brief. The gray of daylight was still pasty on the panes. He felt dirty and sick. The new flannel jacket was a sweaty mass. He peeled it off and hurled it to the floor. The best gray slacks were crumpled like an ocarina. He pulled off the heavy brogues that leaded his feet. They were good shoes; he'd bought them in England. When he had money and position. When the best was none too good for Colonel Steele. He rubbed his fist hard across his upper lip. No tears. He hadn't the strength for tears.

He pulled off the slacks, left them where they fell. A shower would revive him, at least enough to put him on his feet for a few hours, until she came home.

He stayed under the gentle shower for a long time. The water was soothing; even the sound of it was soothing. He'd always, all of his life, loved the sound of breaking water. Nothing that had happened had changed that. The crawling of water over sand, the hush of a word, *no . . . no . . . no . . .* Not even that had changed his love of the power of the sea.

He put off shaving. His hands were trembling when he picked up the razor. He knew what the rasp of it would do to his nerves. Undo the good of the water. Yet he must shave. A man didn't look like just any ordinary man unless he were clean-shaven.

It was almost six o'clock before he was dressed. In the protective coloring of tan gabardines, a white sports shirt. Too late to take the discarded clothes to the cleaners. He wadded them into a bundle and pushed them in the closet. It hurt him to see the navy-blue flannel jacket, the good-looking, high-style jacket, dumped there. He rubbed his lip again. He'd wear it yet. He'd wear it to the best places in town, the places where that kind of a jacket ought to be worn. He was through living in a hole; he was going places and doing things. Big places and big things.

He lit a cigarette and took a deep drag. His head felt light as mist. No wonder—he hadn't eaten since noon the day before, a couple of sandwiches then. He wasn't hungry. His mouth tasted stale as the smoke of the cigarette. He didn't want to go out into

Mel's kitchen, eat the old stuff that had been in the refrigerator for days. If only she would come.

There was no reason to believe that she wouldn't come. Something she couldn't foresee had happened last night. Maybe a job out of town. He hadn't returned to the apartment until almost seven. She must have called him all afternoon, then had to leave without getting word to him. There was no way that she could leave a message. No possible way.

She'd return any minute now. She'd explain as she had the other time—and what had her explanation been? He'd explained to her, but had she ever explained to him? She'd said it was none of his business. She'd talked about the big show she might land. But she hadn't said where she was all night.

She'd meant to. And he'd meant to question her after he explained himself. But the conversation had channeled; they'd never returned to the subject. It didn't mean that she hadn't a simple and reasonable explanation, as she had the night when she'd been caught by her lawyer.

She'd come in pretty soon now. She'd be full of news about the show. There wouldn't be any wrangle tonight; they'd talk it all over, make plans for New York. God, it would be good to be back in New York again! Where no one knew you; where there weren't Nicolais parking on your doorstep. Brub was a great guy—the old Brub. But marriage changed a man. Being a cop changed a man.

The phone hadn't rung all day. It wasn't going to ring now, not while he stood here in the bedroom looking at it. There wasn't any girl worth getting upset over. They were all alike, cheats, liars, whores. Even the pious ones were only waiting for a chance to cheat and lie and whore. He'd proved it. He'd proved it over and again. There wasn't a decent one among them. There'd only been one decent one, and she was dead. Brucie was dead.

Laurel couldn't disappoint him. He'd known what she was the first time he'd looked at her. Known he couldn't trust her, known she was a bitchy dame, cruel as her eyes and her taloned nails. Cruel as her cat body and her sullen tongue. Known he couldn't hurt her and she couldn't hurt him. Because neither of them gave a damn about anyone or anything except their own skins.

He was neither surprised nor disappointed that she hadn't turned up. He'd expected it. He wasn't going to fight with her when she came back; he was going to take her out and show her the town. Whatever she was, she was his. She was what he wanted.

He wouldn't sit around any longer, yenning at the phone. He turned on his heel, half-expecting its ring to summon him back, and he went into the kitchen. The bread was dry, the cheese hard, but he put together a sandwich. His throat closed to the tasteless stuff; he was hungry, he needed a well-cooked dinner, something good to eat, served in style. He threw away most of the sandwich; he couldn't stomach it.

It was after seven, way after, and she hadn't come, hadn't called. He wouldn't wait around any longer. He was hungry. He strode through the living room and out the front door into the blue courtyard. There were no lights in her desolate apartment; she wasn't there. She hadn't been there.

Slowly he went back into his apartment. At the door he sprinted; he thought he heard the phone, but the ringing was only in his mind. The apartment was quiet as dust. She wasn't coming. She hadn't come last night, and she wasn't coming tonight. Only a fool, only a mawkish loon would hang around waiting for her to come.

This time he did quit the apartment, definitely, defiantly. Without leaving a note behind. The car was in the garage. He hadn't had it out for two days. Time it was moving again. The garage doors opened in smooth silence. He backed out the car, left the motor running while he closed the doors after him. Just in case he didn't get back until late. Just in case his garage neighbors, not one of whom he'd laid eyes on, were the kind who'd wonder what a fellow was doing out so late.

He drove over to Wilshire, not knowing where he'd eat. The Savoy, on up Rodeo, Romanoff's, the Tropics. He was after good food, but he didn't want to waste a lot of money on it. Not until Laurel went with him to those spots. There was always the Derby or Sheetz—not for tonight. Neither could fill the hollow within him.

He passed Judson's, and the brilliant lights of the drive-in, Simon's drive-in, glittered ahead. He thought only for a moment, a brilliant gash of thought that splintered his indecision. Quickly he slewed the car into the parking space.

It was a dare, a magnificent dare. He and he alone of those outside the case knew the police were watching Simon's, knew the help was alerted for the face of an average young fellow. It was the kind of dare he needed, to return here openly, to take the chance. Knowing they were watching for a man of a certain height, of a certain look under the garish lights of the circular counter. They weren't looking for a fellow in a big black coupe, shadowed in the twilight of a car. The same fellow and they couldn't know.

Simon's was always busy; even at this early hour cars were circled close in to the carhops' pavement. There were a couple of holes, and he pulled in boldly, cut his lights, and waited for the hop. A middle-aged couple, a bleached blonde and a balding man, were in the car on his right. Two young fellows in the car on his left. He was certain neither was of the police. It would have amused him to smell cop. He was never more certain of himself than when he attacked. Cringing in corners alone was fearful. He was through with that stuff.

The girl who came with a menu and bright "Good evening" was young and pretty, as young as sixteen. Pert nose, blue eyes, long, light brown hair under her ugly brown cap.

He smiled at her. "Hello," he said as if he'd been here often, as if he were one of the regulars. "I'm sure hungry tonight," he told her before she went to service another car. He wanted to be noticed, wanted her to remember him as something usual.

Dust. Lochner and his dust. Dix would have plenty of Simon's Drive-In dust in his car. He lived in the neighborhood; he could eat here often. Even the rich Mel Terriss ate here. Even Laurel Gray.

He wondered what name was on the identification card the girl had left on the outside of the windshield. He wasn't foolish enough to investigate. But he hoped it was Gene, the girl who'd recognized Mildred from her picture in the paper. He wasn't the same fellow.

She returned with her pad, and he ordered steak, french fries, tomato-and-avocado salad, coffee. Cars pushed in and out on the lot. The late diners left and the first show crowd moved in. Constant motion, comings and goings, the countermen too busy to look up, the girl hops too busy running from car to counter to car to know whom they served. He was as safe as in a church.

The food was okay. He flicked the lights, ordered a chocolate shake for dessert. He wasn't in any hurry. He'd give any and all of them a chance to look him over. He wished the police were here to look him over. But he didn't go into the lighted building. He liked a chance, but he was too smart for a risk.

No one paid any attention to him. When he drove out of the lot, no car followed. As soon as he was away from the lights, depression settled on him again. His hands itched to turn the wheel back towards the apartment. She might be there by now, waiting for him. He set the car forward. Let her wait. He'd waited enough for her.

He didn't consciously plan to drive out Wilshire to the sea. But the car was set on its course, and the road led to the dark, wet horizon. The fog blew in at Fourteenth Street, and he should have turned back then. He didn't. He went on, through the opaque cloud, until he had passed into the yellow spray that, falling into a pool, marked the Ocean Avenue intersection.

He knew then what he was going to do. He swung left and pulled in at the curb by the Palisades park. Out of the fog light glow, all things became an indistinguishable blur in the night. He left the car. The fog was cool and sweet as he drifted through it. Into the park, the benches, the trees assuming shape as he neared them. He walked to the stone balustrade. He could hear the boom of the breakers far below, he could smell the sea smell in the fog. There was no visibility, save for the yellow pools of fog light on the road below, and the suggested skyline of the beach houses. There was a soft fog-hung silence, broken only by the thump of the water and the far-off cry of the foghorn.

He drifted through the park on quiet feet, looking for the shape of a living thing, of a woman. But he was alone. The living were huddled behind closed doors, warming their fears of the night in the reassurance of lighted lamps. He came to the corner that jutted out over the cliffs, to the corner which was the beginning of the California Incline. He stood there quietly for a long time, waiting, remembering the night he had stood in the same place almost a month ago. The night he had pretended his hand was a plane swooping through the fog; the night he had seen the little brown girl. He waited, without allowing himself to know why. He kept his hands dug into his pockets, and he leaned over the edge of the balustrade, his back to the avenue. But no bus came to shatter the silence and the fog. There were not even cars abroad, not at this particular time and place.

He tired pretending after a time, and he began to walk, down the Incline, past the mid-hump, pausing there to examine the beaten brush where, in the sunshine of the day, kids took the shortcut down the hill to the beach. It wasn't a good cave, too small and shallow; it offered too little protection from the lights of cars traveling up or down on the Incline. Less protection from the beach road below. There were better places, places of seclusion, of quietness. He thought of the spiny trees in the eucalyptus grove, of the winding road that dipped down into the canyon.

And he walked on, down the Incline to the pool of fog light at the intersection. He didn't hesitate, crossing the deserted road to where the three houses huddled together in the night. He passed them slowly, as if reluctant to accept the closed gates, barring the intruders of the night. He went on to the open lot through which, in sunlight, the beach crowds passed over the broad sands to the sea beyond. He knew where he was going. He sludged through the sand until he stood in front of the third of the huddling houses. It was a tall peaked house, standing dark in the thick fog. He knew this was not the one, the brown girl had entered one of the two gates that stood side by side, the first or the second house.

He scraped through the damp sand to the center house, two stories, both pouring broad bands of light into the fog. There was warmth and gaiety within. Through the downstairs window he could see young people gathered around a piano, their singing mocking the forces abroad on this cruel night. She was there, protected by happiness and song and the good. He was separated from her only by a sand yard and a dark fence, by a lighted window and by her protectors.

He stood there until he was trembling with pity and rage. Then he fled, but his flight was slow as flight in a dream, impeded by the deep sand and the blurring hands of the fog. He fled from the goodness of that home, and his hatred for Laurel throttled his brain. If she had come back to him, he would not be shut out, an outcast in a strange, cold world. He would have been safe in the bright warmth of her. He plowed on up the beach, to where there was no light, where the empty beach clubs loomed in the dark. Groping on, his feet chained in the sand, he stumbled and fell to one knee. He didn't get up again. Instead he slumped down there on the slope of a dune, and he buried his head in his arms.

He was there for a long time. Lost in a world of swirling fog and crashing wave, a world empty of all but these things and his grief and the keening of the foghorn far at sea. Lost in a lonely place. And the red knots tightened in his brain.

He was there for a long time, but there was no time in this sad, empty shell of the night. He was there for so long that he was startled when he heard something running; almost frightened when the small dark shape hurtled upon him. He realized quickly that it was a dog, a friendly terrier. He said, "Hello, fellow," and the dog nosed his hand. He wanted to cry. He said again, "Hello, fellow."

And then he heard footsteps coming over the sand, and he no longer wanted comfort of tears. Excitement charged him; where there was a dog there was a master . . . or a mistress. His hand slowly stroked the dog's curly head. "Nice fellow," he said.

The dog was nuzzling him when the girl came out of the fog. Dix looked up at her and he said, "Hello." She wasn't afraid. She said carelessly, "Hello."

He smiled. She didn't know that behind that smile lay his hatred of Laurel, hatred of Brub and Sylvia, of Mel Terriss, of old Fergus Steele, of everyone in the living world, of everyone but Brucie. And Brucie was dead.

# Chapter Six

## 1

SHE hadn't returned. All night again she had been away. The apartment was empty and cold. He put out the lights before the gray fog of night became the gray fog of morning. He sat there in the dark bedroom waiting for the morning.

He did not dare sleep. Not until he had covered the mistake. The first mistake he had made. The mistake of sand. For sand was an evil and penetrating thing, no matter how much of it you brushed away, particles adhered as if cemented, particles leered where there had been none a moment before. If dust divulged a story, sand screamed its secrets.

It hadn't mattered before. When he could walk away from it, when he need answer to no one. Now uncertainty riddled him. Not knowing how much was in his mind alone, how much was real. It had been a mistake to look up Brub Nicolai, to embrace friendship. If he had remained lone, he wouldn't have had to worry about sand. It was good he was leaving for New York soon. He'd had enough of this neighborhood. He was getting nervous.

It was nothing but nerves. Yet he'd take no chance on sand fouling him up.

He didn't smoke much while he waited. He was too physically exhausted even for that. He could have slept easily, slept long and deep, yet it was not hard to remain awake. His mind was alert. He knew exactly what he had to do and how he would do it. It was only necessary for morning to break. And for no one to come here until after what must be done was done. He did not even want to see Laurel until he was again safe.

Safe. He was safe! He had no fear, no anxiety. He had never permitted fear to engage him. His annoyance at the occurrence of the word safe in his mind reawakened him, and he saw it was morning. He stretched his arms and his body in the first pale gray of light. He felt as if he'd been cramped in a foxhole all night.

He scrubbed his face and hands again, scrubbed his teeth. His suit looked as if he'd lain all night on the sand. That was all right too. He took off the trousers now, put on bathing trunks, and pulled his trousers back over them. The trunks weren't new, he'd bought them when he first came to California. He'd expected to spend quite a bit of the past summer on the beach. But he hadn't had a car, and he couldn't take being packed into an ill-smelling bus or clanging streetcar. His swimming had been done at the community pools in the various neighborhoods where he'd lived. He hadn't had a chance to enjoy the city until Mel's car became available for use.

It angered him that he'd wasted so much time, hanging around public swimming pools and cheap eating houses and neighborhood movies. If he'd known how to get started sooner, he'd be established by now, living high, clubbing with the right people, the people who had money and leisure. There was always room for a good fellow in those circles. For a moment he half-wished for Mel.

The day was lightening, and it looked as if the break for which he'd dared not hope was coming his way. It looked as if the fog was clearing.

He fixed coffee at eight, drank two cups black. He was edgy now. No one ever came to the apartment in the morning, yet the very fact that he was up and about at this hour could draw a passerby. There was yet one more thing he must do before leaving. He was reluctant, not afraid, merely reluctant to bring in the morning paper. Yet for his plan, it must be done.

He didn't get a break on that. The delinquent who delivered the paper hadn't left it on the doorstep. From the living-room window he could see it, not even on the porch but on the walk beyond. He waited at the window until a man he had never seen before hurried out of the patio. An oaf on his way to work, just a little late.

It was the wrong hour for Dix to be up, the hour when the members of Virginibus Arms set out to their jobs. Twice again he started to the door, and each time he was forced to wait until a closing door and retreating footsteps were silenced. He finally opened his door a small wedge and watched from behind it. He could go put on his bathrobe, it would bolster his story of working all night, but he didn't want to waste the time. He was in a nervous frenzy to get away, to do what must be done before it was too late. And there was within him still the fear of Laurel returning. He could not face a scene with her this morning. He hadn't time.

He chose his moment to duck out for the paper. He didn't hurry the act. He made it a matter of everyday business, something a man did without deliberation. He was lucky; he saw no one. But he didn't know how many were watching behind their living-room windows, wondering what the young fellow in Mel Terriss's apartment was doing up so early. Well, he had the answer to that one too. He'd worked all night. Finished his book! That angle hadn't occurred to him before; it was a good one. He'd worked all night, finished his book. He'd been exhausted but too keyed up to sleep. He'd decided to go out to the beach. It wasn't too good a day, but it looked as if it might clear, and there was nothing more relaxing than lying in the sand, listening to the roll of the water. So he'd packed up the manuscript, mailed it on his way, and gone to the beach.

For Christ's sake, for whom was he plotting this minute alibi? He wasn't going to be questioned. He was nuts to think he had to account for his time, as if he were a reform-school kid on parole or a henpecked husband. He didn't have to do a damn thing but climb into bed, take a couple of pills, and get the dreamless sleep he needed. Who cared what he'd done all night and today? Who in hell cared why he'd done it?

The answer was no one, and he certainly wasn't boob enough to proffer an alibi to Brub. He wasn't reaching for trouble; there was only one reason for going to the beach, to put a day, today, on the sand which was in the car and imbedded in his shoes and tucked in unseen crevices of his suit. It wasn't he had nerves; it was because he was smart, because he didn't miss bets.

He had been standing in the middle of the living room, holding the folded paper in his hands. One thing more to do and he did. He opened the paper and looked at the front page.

Relief bathed him, relief flowed gently, excitingly, over him and through him. There was nothing on the front page of the paper, nothing. There was no way he could know what happened. He was off to the beach.

He flung down the paper on the couch, part of it spilled to the floor. Good. As if he'd been reading it. He started for the kitchen, but he hesitated. In case he should run into anyone at the garage, he needed a prop. He pulled out a large manila envelope, gave it bulk with some magazines, sealed it, and carried it under his arm. He needed nothing more. The apartment would tell no story to anyone who came in while he was away. Who the hell was going to come in? Not even Laurel hung around anymore.

He didn't need the prop. He saw no one on his way back to the garage. No one showed up while he was taking out the car. He was on his way. Not as early as he'd expected to start out, but this was better. He wouldn't have to sit so long on the God-damned cold beach.

He had to stop at a post office somewhere along the line. Better to avoid the Beverly one, too much danger of running into Brub. The police station was too near the post office in Beverly. There were Westwood and Santa Monica offices. He decided on the latter; he knew where it was located. There was the danger of hearing rumors, but what if he did? It would make no difference now.

He drove Olympic to Sepulveda, then north to Wilshire, thus avoiding easily the Beverly business district. The road to Santa Monica was a new one by day, even on this dull day with a watery sun trying to break through the overcast. He didn't have to hurry. There was no hurry now, no hurry at all.

He maneuvered the car into the inner lane. There wasn't much traffic at this hour, but he was careful. He couldn't afford an accident or a near accident. He couldn't chance attention from a cop. It annoyed him that such an idea should enter his consciousness, and in annoyance he swerved too quickly. It was luck that nothing went wrong on the swerve. Pure luck. But it meant that luck was with him again. He could stop jittering.

He pulled in at the post office. There were people wandering in and out, like extras in a movie. No one who knew him, no one who would notice him. He addressed the envelope in the car. He hesitated over the address, wanting to make sure that this mail fodder would never turn up again. He rejected sending it to himself either at Mel's, to General Delivery, or back to Princeton. If by any outside chance his mail should be checked, it wouldn't be good. Not in his own handwriting; not in disguised handwriting, too many experts; not from a Santa Monica address. He rejected addressing it to Uncle Fergus or to Mel Terriss for the same reasons. He hit on the solution without particular thought and wrote out the name, a fellow who'd died over Italy a long time ago. The name dribbled into his mind, a simple name, Tommy Johns. The address, General Delivery, Chicago, Illinois. No return address; it would end in the dead letter department, where it wryly belonged.

He took it in to be weighed. The post office was fairly busy. He was third in line at one of the windows. No one knew him; no one noticed him. He paid for the stamps and took the envelope back to a desk as if to write on the return address. The desk he chose had no one at it; he affixed the stamp and mailed the envelope.

Nothing could have been more anonymous than the transaction, yet the palms of his hands were wet when he returned to the car. He'd never had nerves like this; he couldn't understand it. Yet looking at it rationally, it could be understood. He'd been under a terrific strain; that, followed by no sleep, would make anyone jumpy. Before he'd always been able to sleep long and heavily; he'd never had to go through stunts like this. He damned the circumstances which necessitated this stunt.

He was careful to avoid the California Incline approach to the beach; he was taking no chances on getting mixed up with a police inquiry. He drove on down Ocean Front and followed the winding canyon way to the beach. He wasn't the only one who had come for a day on the sands. There were a fair dozen cars parked in the enclosure by State Beach. He parked his own car and went down the concrete steps to the sand.

The beach wasn't crowded. There were a couple of fellows and girls, sweaters over their bathing suits, backed against the concrete wall. They were playing cards, a portable radio giving out music. There was a heavyset man and his scrawny wife farther down the sands. A scattering of young men, singly and together, beach athletes. Dix chose a place against the wall on the other side of the lifeguard station. He took off his coat, folded it, laid it on the sand. He took off his trousers, folded them on top of the coat. He kept his shirt on; the offshore wind was chill under the streaked sky. He took off his socks and shoes, set them aside, and stretched out, his head on his folded suit. The ocean was a hushed sound. The sun was beginning to break through, even faint strips of blue were appearing in the sky. He closed his eyes, and he slept.

On waking, he was amazed. He had evidently dropped into the pit of sleep as soon as he lay down, for he had no memory past that moment. Luck was with him that he hadn't slept too long. It was only a little past three. Discomfort had evidently aroused him, for the afternoon had turned chill; the sky was completely grayed again. Dix shook out his clothes and put them on. Their wrinkles, their sand were legitimate now. The same was true of his shoes and socks. He could take all these clothes to the cleaners not caring who might snoop. He could go home, have a warm shower, clean things, sleep in a comfortable bed.

First he must make certain that he was remembered. He had planned that last night. He drove the car into the gas station across, said to the dark-haired owner, "Fill her up, will you?" and as if in afterthought said, "If you don't mind, I'll phone while you're filling her." The gas-station operator might not remember him, but he could be reminded by the call. He called his own number; when there was no answer, his coins were returned.

The car was ready; Dix drove away. He would have liked to stop at the hamburger stand for food and coffee, particularly coffee. He was chilled from his sleep on the cold sand. But he didn't want to chance running into Sylvia or even Brub; this was their corner. He drove on, winding up through the canyon to San Vicente. There were no eating places on this boulevard, nor were there any drive-ins until he reached Beverly. He had no intention of dropping into Simon's at this odd hour, no intention of forcing his luck. Thinking about food had made him ravenous, yet he could not face going into a restaurant until he'd changed clothes. He wouldn't pass unnoted at any place in Beverly in his doubly wrinkled suit. By now everyone would be babbling about the latest murder. Anything out of line might be suspicious. Anything sandy would be suspicious to the yokels.

He drove on back to the apartment. He didn't want to put the car away; he'd be going out again as soon as he was clean. It was double work putting up the car, yet it meant getting into the apartment without walking openly through the patio. He preferred entering without being observed.

Reviling the need of precautions, he went through the routine. Brake the car in front of the garage, get out of the car, open the garage doors, get in the car, unloose the brake, run the car into the garage, get out of the car, close the garage doors. Doggedly he walked through the alley to the rear door of his apartment. He slowed his walk as he approached. He wasn't unobserved. A yahoo was trimming the hedge just beyond his doors. A little measly Mexican fellow in faded overalls, a battered hat bending his ears, a mustache drooping over his mouth. The shears were bigger than the man. *Clip, clip, clip clip.* The shears chopped with Dix's approaching footsteps. The fellow looked up as Dix reached the back door. " 'Allo," he said brightly.

Dix didn't say hello, he nodded only, and he went into his apartment. He wouldn't have been surprised to find something wrong. He'd been thrown that much off beat by the unexpected gardener. But the apartment was unchanged. The slattern had been in and cleaned, that was all. The coffeepot and cup were clean; the newspaper in the living room was folded on the table. The ashtrays in the bedroom had been emptied; the bed he hadn't slept in was smoothed. Everything was okay.

He restrained himself from looking out to see if the evening paper had come; he knew it was too early. The paper didn't arrive until past five o'clock. He peeled off his clothes, added them to the bundle on the closet floor, and he took a long and hot shower. He shaved without hearing the electricity. He was beginning to feel great. While he dressed—dressed well in a dark tweed, a white sweater under his jacket—he wondered if she would return tonight. Surely she would. She'd been away two nights now. He hoped she would come tonight; he wasn't angry with her. She had a good reason for her absence. He would accept her reason without recriminations. He'd accept anything if she'd just show up, join him for a big feed, come home with him after it.

He decided he might as well wait an hour to see if she'd come. Postponing food had taken the edge off his appetite. He poured a shot of rye, drank it straight. Not that he had need of it, he felt swell. It was a fillip to top his good spirits.

He switched on the radio. Earlier in the day he hadn't thought of that news source. He rolled the stations, but there was nothing but music and kids' adventure yarns; he was between news reports. He turned off the nervous sounds. He preferred the quietness of the apartment.

It was possible the paper had come early. He needed to know what had happened, not have it sprung on him. He opened the door, stepped out, and looked on the porch and walk. No paper. But the Virginibus Arms had suddenly gone in for gardening in a big way. There was another peasant out here in front, doing something to the flower beds. This one was younger, a tall, skinny character, but his face was just as droopy as the little fellow in back. He didn't say hello; he looked at Dix and returned his attention to his spadework.

Dix went back into the living room. If she hadn't shown up by six, he'd go on to dinner. He wouldn't wait around tonight. She definitely must have gone out of town on a job. Probably afraid he'd raise a fuss if she mentioned it in advance. He was pretty sure she'd show up tonight, and he wasn't surprised at all when the doorbell rang. It didn't occur to him to wonder why she'd ring instead of walking in until he was opening the door. And in that split second he was amused by it; she was returning humbly, not on her high horse.

Thus he opened the door and faced Brub Nicolai across the threshold.

# 2

BRUB said, "Hello, Dix." He wasn't smiling; he was standing there, a stocky, foreboding figure.

The cold breath of danger whistled into the inmost crannies of Dix's spirit. He answered mechanically, "Hello."

There was then a moment when neither man spoke, when they remained unmoving, looking each into the other's face. A moment when each knew the other for what he was, the hunter and the hunted.

It was broken when they spoke together, Brub asking, "Aren't you going to ask me in?" and Dix crying, "For Pete's sake, what are you standing out there for? Come on in."

They could feign ignorance of each other's identity after that. They could pretend they were two old pals getting together for a drink. Brub rolled in on his stocky legs, dropped down on the couch, and sailed his hat towards a chair. "I could use a drink."

"Good idea. What'll it be?"

"Scotch. Soda if it's handy."

"There ought to be some around." He stood the Scotch and rye bottles on the small bar, found a soda and opened it. "I'll get some ice."

Brub's voice followed him to the kitchen. "You aren't the two-fisted grogger you used to be, are you? Imagine having two kinds of liquor at your place."

Dix pulled out the ice tray, pressed up the cubes. "You're not such a souse yourself since you grew up, are you, chum?"

But it was hollow interchange. It died before he had the drinks mixed. He tried again, lifting his own highball. "To our youth," he toasted. "Those careless rapture days seem kind of far away, don't they?"

"Like they were of another world," Brub said gravely.

Again silence moved in on them. In the void, he heard the faint plop of the evening paper flung at his door. He couldn't go for it now. Not until he knew why Brub had come. He could even hear far away, or thought he could, the clip-clip of the gardener's shears.

He couldn't take the emptiness which should be filled with man talk. He asked, "What's the trouble, Brub? You look beat."

"You should ask. I am beat."

"I'm asking." He didn't know a thing. He hadn't seen the paper, hadn't heard a radio. He threw a curve, "Is it Sylvia?"

Brub's eyebrows slanted quickly. "What about Sylvia?"

Dix said apologetically, "I thought the last time I was at your place that maybe you were having a little trouble. There was sort of a strained feeling—"

Brub had started to laugh as Dix spoke. It was a real laugh, a laugh at something funny. When Dix broke off, Brub said, "You couldn't be further off the beam. Sylvia is—she's Sylvia." He didn't have to say any more. The whole was in Brub's face and on his tongue and in his heart.

Dix murmured, "That's good." He took another drink from his glass. "What is it then? What's the trouble?"

"You mean you don't know what's happened?"

Dix said with mock exasperation, "I mean I don't know from nothing. I've been out at the beach all day—"

He had only to say "beach" and Brub tightened. He had said it deliberately. He went right on, "I just got in about an hour ago, cleaned up, had a quick one, and settled down to wait for Laurel." He glanced at his watch. "I hope she won't be too long tonight. I'm starved."

"You were at the beach all day." Brub said it with wonder, almost with awe.

It was what Dix wanted. He relaxed in his chair, comfortable in his well-being, enjoying his drink. "Yes. I'd worked all night, finished my book," he threw in with modest pride. "I was worn to a pulp, but I was too high to sleep, so I decided to go out to the beach. Looked as if it might clear—what's happened to the California sunshine? I'm sick of this gray stuff—but it didn't." He took another drink. He wasn't talking too fast or too emphatically. He was rambling like a man enjoying the cocktail hour. No alibi, just discussion of the day. "It did relax me though, enough that I took a nap out there. Wonderful what the briny will do for a man, even on a day like today. I feel like a million dollars tonight." It was exciting to sit there behind the pleasant mask and watch the suspicion simmer out of the hunter.

Brub exclaimed, "Finished the book! That's great. Going to let Sylvia and me have a look at it?" He was trying to reorient his thinking while he made expected talk.

Dix shook a rueful head. "I've already shipped it East. This morning. I'll send you an autographed copy when and if it's published. I promised you one for your help, didn't I?"

"Help?" Brub tried to remember.

"Sure. About tire tracks, and that day you let me go up the canyon with you. I appreciated that."

Brub remembered. Remembered more. Depression settled heavily on him again.

"Now, what's your trouble?" Dix demanded. "Here, let me fix you another." He took Brub's glass. His own wasn't half empty.

He was watching it. With no food and his already high spirits, he didn't need alcohol. He talked while he poured a fairly stiff one. "Tell me what's weighting your strong shoulders." He carried the drink to Brub. "Try this."

"Thanks." Brub looked up at him. "You haven't seen the papers?"

He went back over to the easy chair. "I had a quick look at the *Times* this morning—" He broke off, getting it out of Brub's eyes. "Brub—you don't mean—"

Brub nodded heavily. There wasn't an atom of suspicion left in him. If there ever had been. "Yes. Another one."

Dix let out his breath. He exclaimed softly, in shocked disbelief, "God!"

Brub kept on nodding his head.

"When—where—Was it . . . ?" Dix stammered.

"It was," Brub said grimly. "The same thing."

"The strangler," Dix murmured. He waited for Brub to go on with the story. It wasn't a time for questions, only for shocked silence. Brub would talk; he was too tightly crammed with it to keep from talking. He had to have the release of words.

"It was last night," Brub began. He was having a hard time getting started. He wasn't a cop at all; he was a man all choked up, swallowing the tears in his throat. "Last night or sometime early this morning." His voice broke. "It was Betsy Banning. . . ."

Dix let the horror mount in his face. "Bets . . . the little . . . the girl who looked . . . like Brucie . . ." He didn't have to control his voice.

Anger, the hard iron of anger, clanged in Brub. "I'd kill him with my bare hands if I could lay them on him."

Had Brub come to kill? On ungrounded, fathomless suspicion?

Dix waited for him to go on. Brub was steady now, steadied by the iron anger that was holding him rigid. "Wiletta Bohnen and Paul Chaney found her."

Wiletta Bohnen and Paul Chaney were top picture stars, Bohnen was Mrs. Chaney. The publicity on this one would be a feast to the peasants who got their thrills through the newspapers.

"They walk their poodles on the beach every morning at eight o'clock. Walk from their house—it's the old Fairbanks place—up to the pier and back." Brub took a swallow from his glass. "They didn't see her on the way up. They had their dogs on leash, and they cut across slantwise several houses to the water. But the dogs were running free on the way back. . . . The dogs found her. Almost in front of the Fairbanks house, just a little above the high-tide mark."

It was hard for Brub to talk. He had to stop and swallow his throat more than once.

Dix made his own voice husky. "That's—that's all you know?"

"We know she went out a little after eleven," Brub said angrily. "She had friends there earlier, college friends of hers . . . the boy she was going to marry. She always took her dog out for a run at night, no matter what time it was. Usually it was earlier. She wasn't afraid—she was like Sylvia, the ocean was always something safe, something good. Her father—" Brub swallowed again. "Her father sometimes worried—especially these last few months—but she wasn't afraid." There were angry tears in Brub's eyes. "And she had her dog."

"The dog—"

Brub said jerkily, without intonation, "We found him. Buried in the sand. Dead . . . strangled."

"Poor fellow," Dix said from his heart.

"One thing," Brub spurted with hard anger. "Nothing had happened to her." Then he laughed, a short, grating laugh. "Nothing but death." He said with irony, using that weapon to combat tears, "It's some comfort to her father and the boy—nothing happened to her."

"Was it the same man?" Dix asked dubiously.

"Who else?" Brub demanded belligerently. "It's been just about a month. Every month. Every damn stinking month—" He wiped the back of his hand across his eyes without shame. Then he picked up his glass and drank a third of its contents.

Dix looked at him with sorrow. "God!" he repeated. It was terrific, the most terrific show of all. With Brub here weeping and flailing impotent anger at an unknown, a killer who killed and went quietly away into the night. And Brub would never know.

Dix asked, "No clues?" as if he were certain this defeat too followed the pattern.

"On the sand?" Brub snorted. "No, no clues. No buttons, no fingerprints, no cigarette stubs, no match folders, not even a calling card."

Dix rubbed his cheek. It was apology for a foolish question.

"Mind if I use your phone?" Brub asked abruptly.

"Go right ahead. In the bedroom. Can I fix you another—"

"No. I've got to get on downtown to headquarters." Brub left the couch and went into the bedroom. He didn't close the door. He wasn't going in to snoop; a lot of good it would do him to snoop.

Dix was quiet, deliberately listening to the call.

"Sylvia?"

Dix relaxed but he listened.

"I'm calling from Dix Steele's. . . . No, Sylvia! No, I can't come home yet, I have to go down to headquarters. . . . I dropped in on Dix for a drink and a few minutes rest from . . . Nothing. . . . No. . . . Absolutely nothing. . . . You'll stay there until I come for you? . . . Be sure to wait for me. . . . Good-bye, darling. Good-bye."

Dix didn't pretend he hadn't heard the call. Brub knew that every word was audible in a small apartment. Brub didn't care; he'd left the door open. Dix asked, "Sylvia frightened?"

"I am," Brub said. He walked over and picked up his hat.

"She's not staying alone at night until we catch the murderer."

"I don't blame you," Dix agreed. "Can't I give you a quick one before you leave?"

"No, I'd better not." He seemed reluctant to go, to face the blank wall again. There would be ants scurrying around the wall, with plaster casts and fingerprint powder and chemical test tubes, but it wouldn't change the blankness of the wall.

"Come again, Brub." Dix said it with true urgency. "Come anytime. Anything I can do to help you out—"

"Thanks." He put out his hand, clasped Dix's. "Thanks. You've helped me over a rough spot, fellow. And I'm not kidding."

Dix smiled. The inner smile didn't show, the outer one was a little embarrassed. The way a man is embarrassed at any show of emotion from a friend. "The bottles aren't empty. Come back."

"Oke." At the door, Brub hesitated. "Leaving town soon?"

Dix was surprised at the question. As much as if it had been a police warning. He remembered then, and he laughed easily. "Now that the book's done? Oh, I'll be around a couple of more weeks at least. Maybe longer. Depends on Laurel's plans."

From the doorstep he watched Brub start away. Watched Brub stoop on the walk, and a splinter of doubt again chilled him. But Brub turned back to him at once. "Here's your paper," he said.

He didn't want the paper. He didn't want to look at it. The moment it was opened in his hands, there again in the solitude of his living room, he was sickened. He'd never felt this way before. He hadn't felt this way when Brub was talking about it. Actually he hadn't thought then, he'd been too busy playing the required part.

He didn't want to read about the girl and her dog. He didn't want to look at the smile on her clean-looking, vital face. Even with the same morbid curiosity of the peasants tickling him, he didn't want to read about it. He put the paper down with trembling hands.

He hadn't needed a drink for a long time, not the way he needed it now. He'd had enough. Another might be too much, might be the edge to start him on a binge. He didn't dare go on a binge. He didn't dare anything other than complete alertness in all of his senses.

What he needed was dinner, a big, hearty, tasty dinner. Steak and french fries and asparagus and a huge fresh green salad, then a smoke and coffee and something special for dessert, strawberry tart or a fancy pastry and more coffee.

Hunger ached in him. If only Laurel were here. He knew damn well she wasn't coming; he'd known it all along, but he'd been kidding himself. Teasing himself with hope. Wherever she was, whatever guy she'd gone off with, she didn't think enough of Dix even to let him know. She'd never cared for him; she'd made him a convenience while Lover Boy was tied up with some kind of ropes. Once Mr. Big was loose, she didn't even say good-bye. The old couplet taunted him—*She didn't even say she was leavin'*—and he was furious at its popping into his head. The situation wasn't funny. It hurt. It would hurt if he weren't angry.

Well, he wasn't hanging around any longer waiting for Laurel. He was going to eat. He went fast, strode out the back door, down the alley to the garage. It was annoying to have to go through the whole stupid routine again. He shouldn't have put the car up. Tonight he wouldn't. If the police wanted to pry into the dust, he'd make it easy for them. The car would be at the curb.

There was a young fellow peering into the works of a Chevy in the alley. He didn't turn around to look at Dix. Or to say hello. Dix jutted his car out and drove away fast. He didn't bother to close the garage doors. He hesitated at the Derby, but he wanted something better tonight. Something as good as the Savoy. He could afford it. He had two hundred and fifty bucks, damn near, and he was hungry.

This was the kind of a place in which to dine. These were the kind of people a man wanted to be a part of. People who knew the gentleman who seated you, who spoke to him by name. This was the way he was going to live someday. Nothing but the best. No worry about money. Or about nosey cops.

He ordered a rich meal, and he ate it leisurely, appreciating every well-cheffed bite. He lingered as long as he possibly could. He didn't want to leave this haven. Eventually there was nothing to do but go out again into the thin cold night. The fog had dissipated, but there were no stars in the covered sky. And now? Not back to the unutterable loneliness of the apartment. There was always a movie. He drove down Wilshire slowly; he'd seen the Beverly. He parked around the corner from Warner's. He didn't care what the picture was; it was a place to pass time.

There was a double bill. A mild comedy; a tear-jerking problem story. Neither was absorbing. He could scarcely stay awake during the tear-jerker. But the time was passed; it was midnight when he came out of the theatre. There was nowhere else to go now. The streets of Beverly were quiet as the streets of a nine-o'clock town. Nowhere but back to the apartment.

He dreaded sleep, sleep and dreams. If only she would come back; if only she'd take him and comfort him as she had on that other night. He didn't tell himself a tall tale now, that she might be waiting for him, in all her beauty and warmth. He went into the soda fountain next to the theatre. It was closing, but he didn't care. He gathered a handful of magazines from the stand, the only kind of magazines there, movie stuff, crime stuff. Anything to keep his mind serviced until he was forced into sleep.

He didn't put the car up. It didn't matter who saw him coming in. And he wasn't going out again. If he changed his mind and did want to go out again, it was nobody's business.

He came to a sudden stop just inside the patio. It wasn't lone and desolate, a figment of a blue dream. Someone was there. A dull red circlet was burning in the shadows, back by the rear apartments. For a moment he thought it might be Laurel, but in the silence he heard the flat-paced steps of a man, an unknown man.

Dix covered his pause, stooping down as if he'd dropped something on the ground. Something small that had fallen without sound. Feeling for it until he found it, perhaps his latchkey or a packet of matches. Without another glance to the red circlet, he went to his own place, entered, and shut the door, shut away the menace that might lie in the night. He was breathing heavily.

It was ridiculous to have let the presence of a man affect him simply because there had not before been a man waiting in the shadows. How did he know but that this man had a last cigarette nightly in the patio before turning in? How could he know? He, Dix, always came the back way when he was late. The man might be a musician just home from work, pumping the stale air out of his lungs before bed. Maybe it wasn't a guy who walked nightly; maybe he was locked out tonight and waiting for his wife to get home. Or it could be a guest, somebody's uncle or cousin, who beat the family home. Dix could think up a thousand and one explanations. Any of them good. Any of them stamped with logic. Any except the first one that had hit him, that for some unfathomable reason the man had been put there to find out what time Dix Steele came in. As if anyone would care.

He was all right now. He dropped the magazines on the couch and made for the bar. He'd have a nightcap, a small one before turning in. He was slightly chilled; there was a definite hint of autumn, if only the mildness of California autumn, in the air tonight.

The guy might be, he smiled, a private dick. Somebody's ex might have put him there to see how the lady was behaving. Maybe Dix wasn't the only one wondering where Laurel was keeping herself. There was something funny about the divorce relationship between Laurel and her ex; she was so damn careful to keep men out of her apartment.

He tossed off the drink, gathered up the magazines, and put out the lights in the living room. He needn't worry about the man outside. It wasn't someone interested in— He heard the footsteps then, the flat, muffled footsteps. They were coming this way. Panic squeezed him. Unhurried, inexorable, the footsteps were bringing the man up the portal to Dix's door. Without sound, Dix quickly crossed to the window, flattening himself against the long drape. He could see out; the man could not see Dix even if he stopped and peered into the room.

Dix stood, not breathing, not having breath. Listening, seeing the shadow, the approach of the red dot, the shape of the man himself, a dumpy, shapeless shape topped by a shapeless hat. The man did not pause. He walked past Dix's door and out into the patio, crossed to the opposite portal and started again to the rear.

Dix leaned weakly against the curtain. Within his head his thoughts sounded shrill, falsetto. No one cared what he did. No one cared. No one cared. . . .

He left the window, walked the silent blue-dark room to his bedroom. He didn't put on the lights. He lay on the bed with the darkness broken only by the red dot of his own cigarette. No one cared; Laurel didn't care. She'd gone off without saying good-bye. She'd known, known that night that it was their farewell. He'd almost known it himself—he'd even questioned her. And she'd denied. She'd lied in his face, lied in his arms. . . .

He hated her. She was a cheat and a liar and a whore, and he hated her while the tears rolled from his eyes down his cheeks to salt his mouth. No one cared, no one had ever cared. Only Brucie. Brucie who had gone away leaving him alone, alone for-ever, for all of his life.

He ground out the cigarette. It wasn't ended with Laurel. He didn't end things that way. She'd find that out. She'd come back;

she had to come back. She wouldn't walk off and leave everything in her apartment. Her clothes would be important to her if nothing else was. If no person was. When she came back, he'd be waiting. He'd end it his way, the only way that meant a thing was finished.

## 3

STARTLED out of sleep, he snatched up the phone, with the wild lurch of hope that it was she. The humming of dial tone answered his shout, "Hello." And the long sound of the buzzer brought him fully awake. It was the door, not the phone, which had wakened him.

The door at nine in the morning, with dreams heavy in his mouth and smarting in his eyes. Sometime in the night he had undressed; sometime he had fallen into frightful sleep.

He pushed out of bed. Taking his time. Knowing that nothing of meaning to him could be leaning on the door buzzer at this morning hour. Knowing he did not want to answer the summons. Yet knowing that he must. It might be a wire from her. It might be Brub.

He grumbled, "Keep your shirt on," while he roped the belt of the silken paisley robe about him, slid his feet into the morocco leather scuffs. He plodded into the living room, any man disturbed at his rightful slumbers, making no pretense at a smile as he flung open the front door.

There were two men waiting outside; he had never seen either of them before. One was a portly man in a brown suit, a man with a heavy, inexpressive face and spaniel-brown eyes. The other was a young fellow in gray, a neat-looking young fellow with bright gray eyes. The portly man wore a shapeless gray hat with a faded hatband; the young fellow wore a well-shaped brown fedora. It wasn't that each hat belonged to the opposite suit; it was that they wore hats at all. Men didn't wear hats in Beverly Hills. These men were strangers, strangers with purpose.

The younger said, "We're looking for Mel Terriss."

Dix didn't say anything. He didn't believe what he heard for the moment. It was shock, but it was a dull shock. Whatever he had been expecting, it wasn't this. After a moment he managed to say, "He isn't here."

"This is his place, isn't it?"

"Yes," Dix said. "But he isn't here."

The young fellow looked a little disappointed, or maybe he was perplexed. He seemed to be trying to figure it out. He said finally, "Mind if we come in? I'm Harley Springer." He gestured to his partner. "And Joe Yates."

Dix didn't want them in. He didn't want to talk about Mel Terriss at any time, certainly not now before his eyes were open, before his brain was quick. But there was nothing he could do outside of shutting the door on Harley Springer's foot. The young fellow had it in the door.

Dix said, "Yes, come on in. I'm Dix Steele."

"Looks like we got you out of bed," the big Yates commented. He had a snicker in the corner of his mouth.

"You did," Dix agreed. He wasn't going to get angry at this pair. Not until he found out why they'd come to him. And he wondered if Laurel had set them on it, Laurel with her stubborn determination to get Mel's address. He didn't believe Mel owed her any seven hundred. She'd put that in hoping Dix would think it was important enough to give out with the address. Thinking money would tempt him.

He led the way into the living room. A neat living room, he hadn't hung around it last night. "Sit down," he said. There were no cigarettes in his pocket, none on the tables. He had to have a cigarette. A drink would help too, but he couldn't take a drink at this hour. It wouldn't be a good tale for them to carry back to whomever had sent them. A cigarette was essential.

He said, "Excuse me while I get my cigarettes, will you?" He went quickly into the bedroom, gathered up a pack and his lighter, returned before the men could have had time to walk over to the desk. They were still on the couch, the younger man with his leg crossed one way, the big fellow with his crossed the other. They hadn't moved, only to light cigarettes of their own. He took the chair across from them. He was as much at ease as a man could be, dragged out of bed, entertaining a couple of strangers while he was wrapped in a bathrobe. Entertaining without knowing why. But he smiled at them. "What can I do for you?"

The young one, Harley Springer, took off his hat. As if he should have remembered to do it before. As if he were a cop, someone from the D.A.'s office, not used to taking off his hat when he invaded a man's privacy. He repeated then his first remark, "We're looking for Mel Terriss."

"And he isn't here," Dix smiled.

"Where is he?" Yates flipped.

The young Springer gave Yates a look, a look that meant: Shut up, let me handle this. A look that meant: You're an oaf and this guy's a gent; let a gent handle it.

Dix was actually beginning to feel at ease. He didn't have to worry about being on his toes with Springer and Yates. They weren't that well coordinated; it wasn't like being with Lochner and Brub. He answered Yates as if Yates weren't oafish. "He's in Rio," he told him. "He went down there on some big job. I subleased from him before he left."

The two exchanged a look. Dix waited. Let them explain it. Make them do the talking. He'd changed his mind about these two being cops, more like from a collection agency, trying to get on Mel's trail over those unpaid accounts.

"You're sure he went to Rio?" Springer frowned.

**193**

Dix laughed. "Well, I didn't fly him down and get him settled. But he told me he was going there. I took his word for it. I don't know why he should have told me that if it weren't true." He laughed again. It was his turn now. Time for their explanation. He stopped laughing. "Are you friends of his?" he demanded.

"Nah," Yates said.

Springer gave his partner another shut-up look. He said, "We're from Anson, Bergman and Gorgonzola. Lawyers. Our firm handles Mel Terriss's trust."

It was time to walk softly. He didn't know about trusts.

Springer continued, "We haven't heard from Mel Terriss since July." Evidently it was unusual. The way that Springer said it. "He hasn't even been around for his check."

"He didn't communicate with you from Rio?" Dix showed surprise.

"No. We had no idea he'd gone to Rio until recently. Mr. Anson or Mr. Bergman heard something about it."

Or Mr. Gorgonzola. From an alley cat who'd blabbed, who for some reason wanted to get in touch with Mel Terriss. Bad enough to ask her lawyer about him. Her lawyer and Mel's lawyer. There wouldn't be two Gorgonzolas prominent in legal circles.

"It's strange he didn't communicate with Mr. Anson before leaving. Or since. Particularly since it was Mr. Anson who had so often urged he go there."

Yates said, "Anson thought he might straighten up if he got out of town."

Harley Springer gave a light sigh.

Yates went on doggedly, "Mel's been gassing about getting a job in Rio long as I can remember. Every time he was extra loopy. He never had no intention of going to work."

Springer cut in quickly, "Do you know when he left?"

"He told me I could move in the first of August. He'd be gone before then."

"You don't know by any chance if he went by boat or plane?"

"I don't," Dix smiled slightly. They were going to check passenger lists. "He did say something about going by freighter, a sea voyage to get in trim." He shrugged, widened his smile. "I can't say I believed him. He was too fond of comfort for such rigors." Let them try to check all the freighters that steamed out from the California ports. They'd get nowhere.

He'd had enough of this. He wanted his coffee. He wanted peace. He prodded them, "I'm sorry I can't help you any more than this, gentlemen." He rose. "I didn't know Terriss particularly well. He'd hardly confide his plans to me. I'm a tenant, that's all."

Yates was going to stick his big foot into it again. There was a malicious look in his soulful brown eyes. "The trust pays Mel's rent in advance. To keep him off the street. How'd you arrange to pay him?"

Even Springer's embarrassment didn't quiet the rage in Dix. He smiled wryly, as if it were none of Yates's business to so question a gentleman, but being asked, he would reply. "I gave him a check for a year's rent, Mr. Yates. He said he intended to be away at least that long." This time he was polite but firm. "If that is all—"

He waited for them to rise. Springer made apology. "I'm sorry to have had to bother you, Mr. Steele. You understand it's a job—when Mr. Anson—"

"Or Mr. Bergman or Mr. Gorgonzola," Dix smiled wholeheartedly. "I understand." He didn't include Yates in his understanding. He moved the two men to the door, opened it. Yates went on outside. Springer stopped on the doorstep. "Thanks for your help."

"Little enough," Dix said.

Springer had another question. He'd been holding it, now he sprang it. "What about his mail?"

It came too fast for preparation. But Dix could think fast. He could always think fast in a pinch. "I suppose some has been coming," he said as if it had never occurred to him. "I'll ask my secretary." He laughed. "She keeps everything so efficiently I wouldn't know where to look. I'll tell you, leave your address and I'll have her forward it." He accepted the card from Springer, said good-bye. Yates was already out in the patio, watching the gardener plow up geraniums.

Dix shut the door with a thud. He crushed the card in his fist. Damn snoops. Why should they or anyone care what had happened to Mel Terriss? Stupid, sodden, alcoholic Mel. The world was better off without Mel Terrisses in it. Why should Laurel care? Unless she were trying to get Dix into trouble.

Let them prove, let them try to prove he didn't have a secretary. He'd go through the bills and the ads. Send the harmless ones, the ones without purchases after July. He shouldn't have used the charge accounts, but it was an easy way to do it. So easy.

It was Mel, fat-headed Mel, who was going to run him out of California. Before he was ready to go. Before Laurel came back. He'd be damned if he would. He'd settle with Laurel before he left. They couldn't hang a man for using a friend's charge accounts. Particularly if the friend had told him to make use of them. No one could prove Mel hadn't told him that.

He wanted a drink more than ever; he was so angry he was rigid. Again he didn't dare. At least not until lunchtime. It was legitimate then, not before, unless you were a confirmed alcoholic like your friend, Mel.

He should have asked them about another disappearing client. He should have said: By the by, what's happened to your client Laurel Gray? She's missing too, didn't you know? Maybe she's gone to join Mel.

His face darkened with rage. He flung the crumpled card into the basket. He wasn't going to sit around and be questioned by any lugs who happened by. He'd dress and get out of here. Quick.

But the phone stopped him. The silent phone by his bed. He

sat down, and he dialed Laurel's number. The sound of ringing went on and on until he hung up. She hadn't sneaked back in. There was an idea nagging at the back of his mind; it had been there last night; it was there again now. It had to be faced. Laurel could have moved out of the Virginibus Arms.

He didn't dare go to the manager's apartment and ask. The old bag might start thinking up her questions about Mel. He'd had enough of Mel today. He could go up to Laurel's apartment; that he would dare. But it was pointless; she wasn't at home. She'd answer the phone if she were; she'd be afraid not to, afraid it might be a business call. He picked up the phone book, then laid it down. He wouldn't phone the manager from here. Not and chance having the call traced. Go out to a booth, disguise his voice. Not that the manager would know it, but someone might be around who did.

He was thinking as if it were Laurel the lawyer's narks were asking about. As if it were Laurel's life the cops were prying into. He could ask anything he wanted about Laurel. It was perfectly safe. Yet he didn't pick up the phone.

He was just starting to the shower when the doorbell buzzed again. His fists clenched. It couldn't be those two back again. It couldn't be anything important. Yet he must answer. Slowly he returned to the living room.

There was only one man on the doorstep this time. And he didn't look like he'd come from the cops or the lawyers. He was hatless, coatless, an ordinary guy in pants and shirt. "I'm from the telephone company," he stated.

Dix had the door half-closed as he spoke, "You have the wrong apartment. There's nothing wrong with my phone."

"Yeah?" The man talked fast before the door was further closed. "There's something wrong with the lines running into these apartments. We got orders to check."

"Come in," Dix said wearily. "The phone's in the bedroom." He led the way, pointed it out. "There."

The fellow had a black satchel, like a plumber's satchel. He was going to rasp and ring bells and yell to Joe somewhere on the line. Dix said, "Listen, I'm late. If you don't mind, I'll start getting dressed."

"Sure, go ahead," the man said comfortably. He was already taking the phone apart.

Dix went into the bathroom, closed the door, and locked it. With the shower running, he didn't have to listen to the racket. When he'd finished bathing and shaving, he opened the door. The man was just repacking wire in his little black bag.

"Find any bugs?" Dix asked.

"Not here. Thanks. Shall I let myself out?"

"Go ahead."

Dix lit a cigarette. Maybe there'd been something wrong with his phone. Maybe Laurel had been trying every night to get in touch. It was fixed now, if that were it. That was no longer excuse.

He heard the front door close, and at the same time he heard the clip-clip of the gardener outside the window. If he didn't get out of here, his head would spilt. He hadn't noticed the weather; he'd had too much on his mind. It was still gray, but there were splits of blue in it. Clearing. He put on the same tweeds he'd worn last light. He didn't know where he was going, but he'd be dressed for no matter what. He knew the first stop, the cleaners. With the sandy gabardines and the sweaty clothes in which he'd slept two nights ago, two hundred nights ago. He rolled the bundle of clothes under his arm, left by the back door. The goofy, mustached gardener offered his daily bright saying: " 'Allo."

Dix acknowledged it with a nod, striding on down the alley to the garage. The garage doors were closed. He swung them open. The car wasn't there. It was shock. And then he remembered; he hadn't put it up last night. He hadn't even closed the garage. He began to tremble. With sick anger, sick, frustrated anger. He couldn't pass the gardener again. He'd smash the man's stupid face to a pulp if he heard, " 'Allo."

He walked out of the alley, all the way around the long block to the walk in front of the apartment. The car was where he'd left it. He got in, threw the clothes on the floor, and drove rapidly away. He drove too fast to the cleaners on Olympic. He wasn't picked up. The cops were all out at the beach or hanging around the drive-in. He ought to go up there and eat, see how many he could spot. That would be a laugh. Or out to the beach with the curious.

He dumped the clothes. He'd forgotten he had others here; now he had to drive around with them hung over the seat. He asked for a special on this load, three-day service. In case he left town soon, he wasn't going without that new navy jacket.

He drove on up the boulevard, not knowing where he was going. Not caring. When he saw a corner drugstore, he remembered the phone call and drew up at the curb. There wasn't anyone much in the store—a couple of women at the lipsticks, a few young fellows at the soda counter. Dix closed himself in a booth, looked up the Virginibus Arms number. While he was waiting for the call, he took his handkerchief from his pocket. He didn't hang it over the phone, someone might look in and wonder. But he held it to his mouth, his back turned to the folding door. It would muffle his voice just enough.

The manager's voice was strident to match the strident hennaed head he remembered.

"I understand you have an apartment to rent," he began.

She was as annoyed as if he'd asked for a loan. She not only had all the apartments rented but on long lease. She wondered where he ever got such an idea.

He said, "A friend of my wife's understood that Miss Gray's apartment was for rent."

Her voice was suspicious. "Who said that?"

"A friend of my wife," he repeated. "She said that Miss Gray was moving."

"Well, it's the first I've heard of it. She's paid up—who is this?" she suddenly demanded.

He said, "Lawrence. A. B. Lawrence," reading initials penciled on the wall. He had no idea where the Lawrence sprang from. "Thank you." He hung up before she could ask more. He had what he was after, information. And no one to know he'd called.

He came out of the booth, ordered coffee and a toasted cheese sandwich at the counter. It wouldn't be very good from the looks of the place, but it was better than nothing. While he was waiting, he took a morning paper from the rack. He hadn't had a chance to bring his in from the doorstep.

The murder was still front-page copy. The police were doing the usual, following every clue. Captain Jack Lochner of the L.A. force was working with the Santa Monica force. Captain Lochner was quoted as believing this was another of the strangler murders.

Dix didn't read all the drivel. The L.A. police were rounding up a maria full of known suspicious characters. The Santa Monica police were rounding up beach bums. There was a lot of questioning going on and no answers. No one had noticed any cars parked along the beach road that night. No one had noticed anything. They never did.

Dix finished his poor breakfast and left. There was more blue in the sky now. The sun was bringing warmth into the day. It was nothing to him. It was an empty day, a day to be passed before another night would come. Another empty night, and yet another empty day to follow. He ought to leave town at once, not wait for his clothes to be returned by the cleaner, not wait for a woman who would not come again.

He swung the car over to Santa Monica Boulevard, drove into Santa Monica. He intended stopping at the Santa Fe office, to find out about railroad tickets east. He'd have to hold out enough money for return fare. But there was no place to park, and in irritation he drove away, cutting across to Wilshire. He had no intention of turning west, yet he did. And he followed the avenue to the Incline, down the Incline to the beach road. It didn't look any different. There were no police lines. There were perhaps more cars than usual parked along the street. Yet perhaps not. With the day warming, the beach regulars would be out in force. Dix didn't slow the car. He drove on down the road, turned off into the canyon and back to town.

He didn't realize that he was being followed until he was held by the light at the San Vicente eucalyptus grove. Until he remembered that the shabby sedan that drew up beside him had been behind him when he turned to the beach. Digging back, he knew it had been behind him when he left the drugstore; uncertainly, he remembered seeing it before then. His hands were cold against the wheel. It couldn't be.

And he was right, it couldn't be. The two men in the sedan were ordinary, and the car didn't wait for Dix to turn, it headed out ahead of him on the green. It was nerves, induced by the early morning visit of Springer and Yates, by the irritation of the gardeners and the lineman and forgetting where he'd left the car. You couldn't drive many blocks without running into a shabby black sedan with two men in it. Wilshire was full of like cars right now.

He wasn't being followed. Yet he drove back to the apartment. If there'd been anything he wanted to do, he wouldn't have cared how many cars were following him. But he was tired. Too tired to fight traffic for no reason. He would go home and sleep.

The front gardener had at last finished with Dix's side of the patio. He was leaning against a pillar, laying off with a cigarette. If anyone was hanging around, trying to find out what Dix had done with himself this morning, it was obvious. A trip to the cleaners, here was the evidence. A stop at a drugstore, and if anyone wanted to know what call he'd made there, he'd have an answer. He'd called to see if Laurel was in. On to Santa Monica to the ticket office, but no place to park. The drive down the beach? Simple curiosity. It was legitimate. He wouldn't be the only man in town with curiosity.

He picked up his paper off the walk, let himself into the apartment. He'd forgotten the cleaning woman. She was flicking the dust off the living-room tables as he entered. She was no more pleased to see him than he to see her. She didn't speak; she substituted a surly bob of her head.

He gave her a like bob as he carried his clothes into the bedroom to hang them. Hoping she would have started with the bedroom, but she hadn't. It was still in ugly disarray. He left it abruptly, wanting to snarl at her, to ask her why she hadn't done the bed and bath first. Knowing why, because too often he was asleep at this hour.

Even as he stood there, hating her, the hideous siren of the vacuum cleaner whined suddenly in the next room. He rushed to the doorway. "Get out!" he shouted. She didn't turn off the infernal machine. She only glanced up at him dully. "Get out," he screamed. "Take that thing and get out!"

Her eyes bugged at him then, her slack mouth opened. But she didn't speak. She pulled out the cord fast, gathered her dust cloths, and scurried out the kitchen way. He heard the door bang behind her.

He steadied himself for a moment against the wall. He shouldn't have lost his temper. He was left with a slovenly bed, an unkempt bathroom. He held himself rigid until he had stopped shaking. Slowly he walked into the kitchen and bolted the back door. He knew the front was locked, but he returned to it, made sure. He had to have sleep, undisturbed sleep. Slowly he plodded back to the bedroom, drew the curtains against the sun. He was desperate for sleep.

He tried to pull the bedcovers into some shape, but his hands were witless. He did manage to slip out of his jacket and kick off his shoes before flinging himself facedown, begging for oblivion.

He lay there, trying to quiet his thoughts, pleading to any gods who might heed to give him rest. And he heard it begin, *clip-clip, clip-clip*. Outside his windows, *clip-clip, clip-clip*. His breath hissed from between his set teeth. It had begun and it wouldn't stop. It would go on, louder and louder, sharper and sharper. He began to tremble. He wouldn't dare order the man away; he couldn't risk having another employee run to the manager with tales. He tried to stop up his ears with his tight fists; he sandwiched his head between the pillows; he tried to will his ears to close. But the inexorable rhythm continued, *clip-clip, clip-clip*.

He began to weep. He couldn't help it. He tried to laugh, but tears oozed from his smarting lids. His whole body was shaken. He twisted the covers in his clenched fists. He couldn't stand it. He'd go crazy if he lay here longer.

Shaking, he moved into the living room, dropped weakly on the couch. He thought he could still hear the shears, but he couldn't. It was only echo in his brain; it would go away. If he closed his eyes, lay quietly, it would go away. His hand fell on the newspaper; he'd dropped it automatically on the couch when he came in with the cleaning. He didn't want to look at it. He knew what it said. He knew all about it. But he found himself opening the sheet, staring at the black headlines. He'd read the story once, but he found himself reading it again, reading every word, every tired word. Strength returned to him, and he crushed the paper, hurled it across the room. He turned over on the cramped couch, turned his back to the room, clamped his eyes as tightly as his teeth. He must find sleep.

Even as he turned, the door buzzer began its sickening rasp. He ignored the first three drones. Lying there rigidly, willing whoever it was to go away. The buzz continued, in longer pressings now, like a drill boring into his tortured head. Whoever it was had no intention of going away. Whoever it was knew that he was within. There was to be no sleep. It didn't matter now. Even the need of it was no longer alive. He got up and padded in his sock feet to the door. He opened it without hesitation. He didn't care who was outside.

Two men. Two men in plain suits and hats and shoes, plain faces to match. Two quiet men. Before either spoke, he knew them for what they were.

# 4

HE STOOD aside to let the men come in. He refused to know why they were here.

One of them said, "Mr. Steele?"

"Yes?"

One of them said, "Captain Lochner sent us to see if you'd mind coming up to the station, Mr. Steele."

He had no defenses. He said, "Certainly not." No matter how pleasantly it was offered, it was a command. "Will you wait while I get my jacket?" He felt naked without his shoes; he was ashamed to mention them.

"Take your time," one of the men said. He was the one who moved over to the desk as Dix left the room. The other one moved to the windows.

He put on the tweed jacket, pushed his feet into the brown loafers, brushed his trousers with his hands. They weren't badly wrinkled, not as they would have been had he slept. His hair was tousled. He took time—they'd said take your time—to brush it. Cigarettes, in his pocket. His lighter—it wasn't his, it was Mel's, narrow, gold, real gold. No initials, no identification. He slipped it into his pocket.

The two plain men turned to meet him. They let him lead the way out of the apartment, walked beside him casually, not one on each side, not clamping his arms. The car at the curb was a plain sedan, not a police car. One of the men said, "Maybe you'd rather follow us in your own car."

Dix caught his breath. He didn't understand; they couldn't be offering him a getaway. He couldn't get away. Not in the fastest car made. He could delay them, but he couldn't escape them.

He said, "It doesn't matter."

"You might as well take yours. You know the way?"

"Sure." He didn't get it. And he didn't like it. It wasn't until he was following them up Beverly Drive that he did get it. This wasn't an arrest. How could it be—they had no charge to place against him. They hadn't a thing on him. But this did put his car into their hands where they could get their God-damned dust. He had to laugh at that. Little good the dust would get them. And if they took casts of the tires while he was in the office, little good that would do them.

The laugh had picked him up. Enough so that he felt himself as he parked across from the station. The two plain men had pulled up just beyond him. Not in the police drive. He joined them to cross the street. He didn't ask what Lochner wanted. He could have now, but it might point up his silence before. Therefore he was silent, going along with them into the flowered grounds, up the stone steps, beyond the door flanked by the great bronze lamps holding green light.

He showed his ease by knowing the way to the office. He was certain it would be the private office; it was. He was surprised to find that Lochner wasn't alone, to find Brub there with him. Somehow he hadn't expected Brub to be in on this. His hands twitched slightly. Why hadn't Brub come for him instead of sending the two zombies? Nevertheless, he gave Brub a wide smile as he spoke, "Good afternoon, Captain Lochner. You wanted to see me?"

"Yeah. Sit down."

Dix sat down, and he calmed down; this wasn't Brub's show. Lochner was the boss. Brub looked like a clerk sitting there at the table surrounded with papers. Dix didn't see the plain men leave the room; he only realized they had gone when they were gone.

Lochner gave him a chance to settle down. The Homicide chief was as drab as before, as tired of it all. He waited for Dix to light a cigarette before he spoke. "Thought maybe you could help us, Mr. Steele."

Dix lifted his eyebrows. He didn't have to pretend to be puzzled. "I'd be glad to. But how?"

"It's that Bruce case."

His hands didn't twitch. He lifted his cigarette calmly to his lips.

"Nicolai told you something about it."

"Yes." He might have spoken too quickly. He added, "You mean the English case?"

"Yeah. You knew the girl?"

"Yes." He directed a small glance at Brub. "We both knew her. A wonderful girl." Lochner was waiting for him to say something more. Dix didn't fumble. There were several things he could have said. He chose a surprised one. "Are you taking over that case, Captain Lochner?"

"Uh-uh," Lochner said. "But I got to thinking—"

Dix nodded. "Brub told me your idea. It could have been the same man."

"I got a list." Lochner rooted out a paper from under Brub's hands. "These men were friendly with the Bruce girl. All Americans. All in England when it happened. Now I wonder if you'd look it over." He held on to the paper, swinging it in his hand. "Just read it over, see what you can remember about these men. Anything they might have said or done. Anything you can remember, no matter what it is." He pushed the paper at Dix suddenly. "Here."

Dix got up from his chair, walked to the table. He didn't look at the list as he carried it again to his chair. There was a trick in this. Some kind of a trick. He hadn't been called in to look over a list. He took his time studying the names, keeping his expression grave, thoughtful. Time to think. To get ready for questions. When he was ready, he smiled up at Lochner, moved the smile to Brub. "My name's on it," he said.

"Yeah," Lochner nodded.

Brub said, "But you'd been transferred before then, Dix. I told Jack."

"My transfer wasn't completed until after I returned from Scotland," Dix explained, as if surprised that Brub didn't know. "I had a month's leave, accumulated." Brub hadn't known. Brub had been shipped out before the changes.

"You came home after that?" Lochner asked.

"No," Dix answered. Walk softly. "I was sent to Paris and into Germany. On the cleanup. I was overseas another year." Say nothing of the months in London. He'd been proud of the cushy job. Adjutant to the general. Say nothing. Lochner was too snoopy. Dix's war record was none of his business.

"Then you saw something of those men?"

He couldn't deny knowing the names. Brub knew them too. They were, most of them, part of the old gang. Some he'd liked; some he'd have liked to kick in the teeth. For instance, Will Brevet. If Brub weren't sitting here, he could send Lochner looking into Brevet. But with Brub present, he couldn't. Brub knew the louse had tried to grab off Brucie.

Dix shook his head. "I'm sorry, but I didn't. I was transferred immediately after my leave. I didn't run into any of these men after I left." Sure he'd run into Brevet in London; he'd even pubbed with him one lonely night. He could lie about that. Lochner wasn't going to track down all these guys.

Whatever the purpose of this summons, it wasn't to look into the whereabouts of a bunch of harmless guys or of Will Brevet. It was funny, in this small world, that Dix hadn't run into any of them after he left London. Not even after he got back to the States. But that was how it turned out, even in the small world.

He walked over and handed the list back to Lochner. He faced the chief squarely. "I don't know a thing against any man on this list. They were all swell guys. There isn't a one of them that could have had anything to do with—with what you think." He'd delivered the defense stirringly; he meant what he said. Brub's eyes applauded. "Is there anything else?" Dix asked quietly.

"That's all." Lochner's big forefinger rubbed over the names. "I guess that's all, Mr. Steele." For a moment, his eyes weren't sleepy. "You can't blame a guy for trying," he said.

He took his list then and walked out of the room, through a communicating door. Dix looked at Brub.

Brub tilted back his chair. "I've tried to tell him. He wouldn't take my word for it." He brought the chair forward again. The legs hit hard on the floor. "You can't blame him for trying. Even if the administration weren't riding him, he'd feel the same. It's a personal failure. That these things could be happening while he's the chief."

Dix sat on the edge of the table. "Yes, I can see how he'd feel." He took out another cigarette, lit it, pushed the pack to Brub and held the lighter. Held the lighter right under Brub's nose. "It's hard lines. For you too."

"We'll get him," Brub said. There was fight in him, no defeat now.

"Keep me posted. I'll want to know how you brought it off. The tec who solved the perfect crimes."

"They aren't perfect," Brub said softly. Then he turned his head fast to look at Dix. "You're going back East soon? Thought you said you'd be around some weeks more—or months."

"I may have to take off sooner than I expect," Dix grimaced. "The beckoning hands of business."

"Don't just disappear," Brub warned. "I want to give you an aloha ball. That'll bring you back."

"I'll make my farewells." He slid off the table. "I won't take up any more of your valuable time now, Brub. Give me a ring and we'll have lunch or dinner in a day or so. How about it?"

"Sure." Brub walked with him to the door. When they reached it, he asked, "How was Scotland?"

He'd forgotten that tangent. It took him a minute to balance the question. He answered, "It was wonderful."

"I didn't know you traveled there."

"Yes." He was thinking about it, not the way it was, the way he'd wanted it to be. "She loved it so. She talked so much about it. It was everything she said." And she was dead, but no one had known. Brub was thinking, And Brucie was then dead, but Dix hadn't known.

Dix lifted his shoulders, lifted the memory away. "So long, Brub." He didn't look back; he let Brub remember him as a strong man, a man who could, after a first shock, keep his sorrow in check.

He'd carried the whole thing off well. If Lochner had been playing a hunch, he'd lost his wad. He knew now there was nothing to get out of Dix Steele. There was nothing damning in being in Scotland when Brucie died. There was nothing damning in having been in London afterwards. Except that he'd told Brub he knew nothing of what had happened. He might have been expected to know from London. Actually, there'd not been a thing in the papers to tie unrelated crimes with the death of Brucie. He'd never seen Brucie's name in print. But he didn't want to go into such explanations; they sounded like alibis. He had no alibis; he needed none.

The car was where he'd left it. If the police had gone after dust, they hadn't taken much. The floor mat was no cleaner than it had been. He felt swell, only he was hungry. It was too early for dinner, not more than a bit after four. A big delicatessen sandwich and a bottle of beer wouldn't spoil his dinner. Not after the starvation wages he'd been on today.

He was lucky, finding a parking place directly in front of the delicatessen. He was always lucky. He ought to kick himself for the megrims he'd had these last couple of days. Something must be wrong with his liver. Or perhaps he was coming down with a cold. From that nap on the beach. Actually he knew what was wrong. It was having Laurel walk out on him. If she'd been around, he wouldn't have had a case of nerves.

He ordered salami and swiss on rye with his beer. Someone had discarded an afternoon paper in the next booth. He reached out for it, folded it back to its regular paging, first page first. The story was still on first. The police had given up questioning the fiancé and the college friends and the father; they were satisfied none of them knew any more about the Banning case than did the police themselves. The police were talking fingerprints now. That was a lot of eyewash. Sand didn't take fingerprints.

Lochner was probably having the force develop fingerprints off that piece of paper right now. Because Lochner would be thorough. Or maybe he'd had them lifted off the steering wheel. You could get dandies off a steering wheel. Only trouble was, he had nothing to match them up with. A beachful of sand.

Dix enjoyed the sandwich. The beer tasted fine. So good that he considered another, but he didn't want to hang around here. The phone might be ringing at the apartment. Laurel might be waiting there. He bought a couple of bottles to take out, and he hurried away. His luck had turned, and that meant Laurel was coming home.

He was left-turning off the drive when he caught sight of the car. The same shabby black sedan with the same two average men in it. He was certain it was the same. He slowed his speed, eased his car around the block. He drove the entire block, and the car didn't show up behind him.

Rage flushed him. It was reasonless to imagine such things now. He'd come through the interview with banners flying; he'd had a good snack; all the indications were that luck had caught up with him. He couldn't revert, even for an imagined moment, to the weaknesses of these last days. He wouldn't let it happen.

As he was crossing the intersection, he saw the car again. It hadn't followed him around the block. It had come the other way to meet him. It followed him to the apartment. It was almost as if the men didn't care if he knew they were following. As if they wanted him to know.

When he parked in front of the apartment, the other car plodded past. He didn't get a good enough look at the men to recognize them again. They didn't have faces to be remembered: they were background men, familiar only in their own setting, in the front seat of an old sedan.

Slowly he entered the patio, thinking, trying to understand. He'd passed Lochner's examination; he was sure of it. Why should he still be followed? He hit on an explanation: the men didn't know it as yet; Lochner hadn't had time to call them off. He took a deep breath of relief. Luck hadn't defaulted. She was still along with him.

Automatically he raised his eyes to the balcony. He stopped short, his eyes widening in disbelief. The door to Laurel's apartment was ajar. He didn't think about who might be watching, he didn't care. Laurel had returned.

He covered the patio quickly, ran up the stairs, reached the door in seven-league strides. He was about to tap, but he let his hand fall. He'd walk in on her, surprise her. He still carried the sack of beer. They would celebrate.

Softly he entered the small foyer, moved through the arch

into her living room. It was better than Mel's living room; she'd had an even better decorator. It was as exciting as Laurel herself, silver-gray and gold and touches of bronze; in this room Laurel would glow. It had been fitted to display her as a Reingold window displayed a precious jewel. The room was empty. But the apartment wasn't empty; he could hear the water running in the bath. She'd come home! She was getting bathed, and then she'd dress and they'd have a swell evening. He was so excited that he couldn't have called out to her if he'd wanted. But he wanted to surprise her. He set the beer down on the couch, carefully, so that the bottles wouldn't clink. And he started softly towards the bedroom door.

He passed the piano, a magnificent baby grand of a strange, bronze-looking wood. The piano had caught his eye before. It was meant to. He must have noticed the photograph, but he hadn't seen it. He'd taken it for granted, a picture of Laurel or of someone in her family. It wasn't. He saw it now. A too handsome, patent-leather-haired gigolo, smiling his too pretty smile, holding the inevitable cigarette wisping smoke. It was a theatrical photo, and it was inscribed in bold and banal theatrical style. "To the only one, the wonderful one, Laurel. With all the love of Jess."

Dix was turned into stone. He knew he had been turned into stone; he was fully conscious of it. The heaviness, the coldness, the roughness of stone. He was perfectly normal otherwise. He could think more clearly than ever. This photograph wasn't something old, someone discarded. It still held the place of honor. Nor was it something new. Not that new. The look of the ink wasn't that new.

He was surprised that stone could have movement. Movement that was noiseless. He entered the bedroom, her bedroom, as lush, as feral as she. From the dressing table, that face smirked at him. From the bed table, that face leered. From the chest of drawers, whichever way her eyes would lift on waking, she could see only that face. As if the man were a god, her household god. And she'd cheated on him! She'd cheated even on her god.

The sound of running water had ceased in the bathroom. There were only little sounds, the gathering up of towels, the closing of a medicine cabinet. He stood there waiting.

# Chapter Seven

## 1

WHEN the door opened, he was as silent as stone; only his eyes had movement. The door opened, and the cleaning woman came out. She took one look at him. Her face twisted; her voice was shrill. "What you doing here? Don't you look at me like that! Don't you yell at me!" She lifted the bath brush, threatened him.

He spoke with quiet dignity, "I thought Miss Gray had returned." He turned and stalked out, leaving her standing there brandishing the brush. He stalked out of the apartment. But he picked up the beer as he passed the couch. He wouldn't leave it for the vicious old harridan.

He didn't relax until he was within his own apartment. The hag would go running to the manager. Sniveling about a man yelling at her, about a man following her to Miss Gray's apartment. A certain man. The one in Mr. Terriss's apartment. He wouldn't deny he'd spoken to her sharply. Not yelled at her; a gentleman didn't yell at a charwoman. He'd spoken to her courteously, asked her not to use the vacuum cleaner this day. That was perfectly reasonable. He wasn't the only man who couldn't stand that infernal din. As for his following her to Miss Gray's apartment, that was absurd. He'd gone upstairs to see if Miss Gray had returned from her trip. He would deny, of course, that he'd entered the bedroom. He had been in the living room when the char appeared and started berating him. His word was certainly better than that of a desiccated old hag.

He put the beer on ice. He didn't want it now. He was cold, too cold. He poured a shot of rye. To warm him, for no other reason. He didn't taste it when it went down his throat.

There had been another man all along, a man she loved, the way Dix loved her. Perhaps the way in which her husband had loved her. There had always been this other man. She couldn't marry him. Henry St. Andrews had fixed that. It explained her bitterness against St. Andrews. She couldn't marry Jess because he didn't have enough money to give her what she wanted. She didn't love even Jess enough to give up the luxury she'd learned with the rich man.

Why had she played Dix? Why had she given him what she had? Where had Jess been then? Dix rocked his head between his tight palms. Why? She alone could tell him; if there'd been a lovers' quarrel, if Jess had been on tour, if she and Jess had decided to split up and do better for themselves. But it hadn't worked. She'd gone back to her love, her little tin god.

And after she got into it with Dix, she'd been afraid to tell him. Because she knew him too well. Because she knew that he wasn't a man to give up what was his. She had been his; brief as it was, in that time, she had belonged to him. She'd even cared for him. He knew it; he wasn't fooling himself on that angle. That was the hardest part of it to face. She had cared for him. The way in which Brucie had. But he'd been second best. He'd been good enough only if the number one was out of the way.

He sat there while the early twilight dimmed the room. Sat

there and hurt and bled until he was again cold and tough and un-yielding as stone. Until even the hot blade of anger gave him no warmth.

He sat there trying to understand. So many things. Why he had been born to live under the rules of Uncle Fergus. Why he couldn't have had what Terriss had, what St. Andrews and the Nicolais had without raising a finger. Why Sylvia had distrusted him. From the first moment he'd walked into their house, he'd known she raised a barricade against him. Why? Why had she been suspicious of him, without any faint reason to arouse her suspicion?

Brub had said it once: Sylvia looks underneath people. Yet how could she see what was beneath the façade? Brub had not been suspicious; even now Brub didn't trust his suspicion. Yet Brub listened to Sylvia and passed it on to Lochner in line of duty. How could they suspect him? He could open the pages of his life to them; they would find nothing there. Why, why should they suspect?

There were no slips, no mistakes. There had never been. There would never be. He had no fear, no reason to fear. They could not hold him. He would go back East. He'd get the trunk off to-morrow by express. He'd go by plane. He'd tell Brub good-bye. Good-bye, Brub; good-bye, Sylvia. Thanks for the buggy ride.

He could find a room, not too far away, a room to hole up in for just a few days. Once he was gone, Laurel would come back to her apartment. He'd be in the shadows watching. He'd take care of Laurel before he actually left town. He would take care of Laurel.

The room was dark now. He sat there in the heavy darkness. His fingers ached, clenched in his hands. His head was banded with iron. He'd been hounded all of his life by idiot fate. He'd had to smash it in the face to ever get anything good. He wasn't licked. He could still smash, walk over the broken pieces, come up bigger than ever. Bigger and smarter and tougher than anyone. He was going to get what he wanted. He was going to have money, and he knew where he was going to get it. Once he had his hands on the money, there'd be no more second best for him. He'd be the top man wherever he wanted to go. No one would put him in second place again.

While he sat there, he heard the steps in the patio. He swung around quickly and looked out. It wasn't Laurel. It was some man coming in from the office, briefcase in hand. The man entered one of the apartments across the court.

Tonight Dix would watch. Tonight she might come. Because he'd been cleared by the police; he'd even cleared himself with the lawyers she'd set on him. Because no one need be afraid of him tonight.

He watched. A man and woman went out, dressed to the teeth. A couple of fellows went out talking about their dates. Another man and a petulant woman who railed at him for being late. It was Saturday night. Everybody going out, putting on the dog, Saturday night out.

He watched the mist begin to fall over the blue light of the patio. To fall and to hang there, listlessly, silently. He waited there in his dark room, behind the dark window. Waited and watched.

His anger didn't diminish. Not even when the hopelessness of his vigil filled him as mist had filled the patio. Even then the spire of his anger was hot and sharp. Yet so heavily did the hopelessness hang on him that the sound of a woman's footsteps wasn't communicated to his anger until she was within the patio. High pointed heels. Slacks, a careless coat over the shoulders, the color washed out by the blue mist. A scarf to mask her flaming hair. He moved swiftly, moved before recognition was telegraphed to his anger. He was out the door, softly through the shadows.

He came up behind her just as she reached the steps. "So you decided to come back," he said quietly.

He had startled her. She swung around in quick terror. It wasn't Laurel. He looked into the face of Sylvia Nicolai. "What are you doing here?" he asked. And he saw that he was not mistaken; this was the very coat that Laurel had worn so often. It had the feel of her coat.

Sylvia shrank away from his touch. She didn't answer him. Fear alone spoke from her wide blue eyes.

"Where's Laurel?" He demanded again, still softly but more sharply, "Where's Laurel? What have you done with her?"

Sylvia was caught there, backed against the step. She wanted to move away from him, but she couldn't; she was trapped. She found her voice. "Laurel's all right," she said gently.

"Where is she?" He caught her shoulders. His hands tightened over them. He held her eyes. *"Where is she?"*

"She—" Her voice failed. And then swiftly she moved. She twisted, catching him off guard, breaking through. Leaving the coat in his hands.

He turned. She hadn't run away. She hadn't sense enough to run away. She was standing there, only a slight distance from him, there by the blue pool. Her breath was coming in little gusts. She spoke clearly, "She isn't coming back, Dix. She's safe. She's going to stay safe."

He unclenched his hands, and the coat fell. It lay there on the ground, slumped there. He said, "You've poisoned her against me. You've always hated me. From the beginning you hated me." He took one step towards her.

She backed from him. "No, Dix. I've never hated you. I don't hate you, even now."

"From that first night, from the beginning—" He was about to step towards her, but she was ready for him. He didn't move. He wouldn't warn her when he moved again.

"From the beginning I knew there was something wrong with you. From the first night you walked into our living room and looked at me, I knew there was something wrong. Something terribly wrong."

He denied it. "You didn't know. You couldn't know." Neither had to fill in; both knew they spoke of the same terror. He jeered, "You were jealous. Because you wanted all of Brub. You didn't even want a friend to have a part of him."

She didn't get angry. She shook her head, a little sadly.

"But that wasn't enough. You had to take Laurel from me too. Because you hated me so."

She spoke now. Without emotion. "Laurel came to Brub. Because she was afraid. Afraid of the way you looked at her. That night she asked you to take her to the drive-in."

He gripped his hands. "And you lied to her."

Sylvia ignored him. "It wasn't the first time she'd been afraid. But it was beginning to grow. Every time she spoke of Mel—"

"Damn Mel!" he cut in.

"What happened to Mel?" Her voice lifted. "Where is he? Without his car—and his clothes—without the cigarette lighter Laurel gave him, the cigarette lighter he wouldn't let out of his hands?"

He watched her, watched her in her little moment of triumph.

"What happened to Brucie?" she went on, softly now. "What happened to the girl who drank coffee in the drive-in with you? What happened to the girl in Westlake Park, to the girl who let you take her to the Paramount, to the girl on Spring Street—"

He broke in again. It didn't sound like his voice when he whispered, "I'm going to kill you." He leaped as he spoke. He didn't telegraph the movement, and he was on her, his hands on her throat before she knew. It was his hands that failed him. Because they were shaking, because before he could strengthen them enough, she was screaming and screaming. By the time he'd throttled the scream, the men were running to close in on him. One from the patio entrance, one from the shadows beyond the steps, one from the shadows behind him. He didn't release his grip, not until he saw who it was running full towards him. Brub. And Brub's face was the face of a killer.

It was Sylvia who saved Dix. Because she whirled and went into Brub's arms, clung to him, keeping him from killing. She wasn't hysterical. What she cried was bell clear. "It worked," she cried in her husky voice. "It worked!"

THEY took him into his own apartment. Into Mel's apartment. Brub and Sylvia, although they didn't want Sylvia to come. They wanted to protect her from the ugliness they expected. Brub and Sylvia and Captain Lochner who had come from the shadows. The shapeless man with the cigarette who had come from other shadows. And the two cops who had driven him to the Beverly station earlier today. They'd come from somewhere.

They turned on the lights, and they sat him down on his own couch. They stood around him like vultures, looking down on him, looking down their noses at him. All but Sylvia. They stood between him and the chair where Sylvia was huddled.

Lochner said, "I'm arresting you on suspicion of the murder of Mel Terriss."

He laughed. He said, "Mel's in Rio."

Lochner went on, "And suspicion of the murder of Mildred Atkinson."

He laughed again.

"And suspicion of the murder of Elizabeth Banning."

They didn't have anything on him. Not a thing.

"And the attempted murder of Sylvia Nicolai."

He hadn't hurt Sylvia. He'd lost his temper over her vicious taunts, but he hadn't done anything to her. A good lawyer would take care of that one.

"Have you anything to say?"

He looked straight at Lochner. "Yes. I think you're crazy."

The shapeless man said, "The girls were safe in August. You killed Mel Terriss in August, didn't you?"

"Mel Terriss is in Rio," Dix sneered.

It was Brub who began talking to him as if he were a human being. "It's no use, Dix. We have Mildred Atkinson's fingerprints in your car. There's only one way they could get there."

Brub was lying, trying to trap him. They hadn't had time to take all the fingerprints out of that car while they talked with him today. They had time to take them while the car stood in the garage or at the curb, while a gardener guarded each door of the apartment by day, while men in the shadows watched the doors at night.

"We have the dust—"

He'd covered the dust. His lawyer would make a monkey of the dust expert.

"—lint from the Atkinson girl's coat—"

His eyes lifted too quickly to Brub's impassive face.

"—hairs from the Banning's Kerry blue on the suit you took to the cleaners this morning—"

You couldn't think of everything. When you were rushed. When your luck had run out.

For one moment the old Brub broke through the deadly, grim-visaged cop. The old Brub cried out in agony, "For God's sake, why did you do it, Dix?"

He sat there very quietly, trying not to hear, not to speak, not to feel. But the tears rose in his throat, matted his eyes. He could not withhold them longer.

He wept, "I killed Brucie."

# About the Author

FROM the tender age of six, when she first learned to write words, Dorothy B. Hughes knew that she wanted to be a writer. Born Dorothy Belle Flanagan on August 10, 1904, in Kansas City, Missouri, Hughes began her writing career as a journalism major at the University of Missouri, earning a bachelor's degree in 1924. She went on to do graduate work at the University of New Mexico and Columbia University, in New York City. For several years she worked as a journalist in Missouri, New Mexico, and New York.

Hughes's first foray into non-journalistic writing was a collection of poetry called *Dark Certainty*, which was published in 1931 and received an award from the Yale Series of Younger Poets. The following year she married Levi Allen Hughes. They would go on to have four children. Later that decade she penned a history of the University of New Mexico called *Pueblo on the Mesa: The First Fifty Years of the University of New Mexico* (1939).

In 1940, she turned to crime fiction, publishing *The So Blue Marble*, her first novel. Critics were immediately impressed with Hughes's clean, understated style and gripping plot. This crisp writing was in part a result of intense editing: her first editor demanded a cut of 25,000 words from the first manuscript and eliminated many of the story's more far-fetched elements. This editing served her well, and she learned to bear down and write carefully and economically in future novels.

After her first mystery novel was published, Hughes wrote regularly, producing roughly a novel per year for the next decade. Three of her books were made into movies—*The Fallen Sparrow* (1942); *Ride the Pale Horse* (1946); and *In a Lonely Place* (1947), widely considered her most powerful book. Several leading Hollywood actors starred in her films, including John Garfield in *The Fallen Sparrow* (RKO, 1943); Robert Montgomery in *Ride the Pale Horse* (Universal, 1947); and Humphrey Bogart in *In a Lonely Place* (Columbia, 1950). This era—the 1940s through the early 1950s—became Hughes's heyday, during which time she was widely considered the most successful female crime writer of the day.

At the pinnacle of her career Hughes abruptly stopped writing novels. She found that her personal life required her mental and physical energy to the point where she could not focus properly on fiction writing. Her mother was ill, and she was caring for her grandchildren. As a result she gave up writing mystery novels. However, she continued to write literary criticism for many years; from 1940 to 1979, she reviewed mysteries for the Albuquerque *Tribune*, the Los Angeles *Times*, the New York *Herald-Tribune*, and other newspapers. In 1978, she was named a Grand Master by the Mystery Writers of America for her entire body of work, both mystery fiction and literary criticism.

Hughes lived most of her life in Santa Fe, New Mexico, and

the West and Southwest were the background for many of her novels. The author also wrote occasional short stories for publications including *Saint, Ellery Queen's Mystery Magazine,* and *Cosmopolitan.* She died of complications from a stroke on May 6, 1993, in Ashland, Oregon.